THE
PICTURE
KNITTING
BOOK

THE
PICTURE
KNITTING
BOOK

ROSALIE LANE

d&C

David & Charles

I dedicate this book to Rita "Toots" Russell-Jones
who combined being both my mother and my biggest fan
and I only wish she could have lived to see it.

Title page: Christopher, Ben and Hannah wearing a
selection of crew neck, rib bottom jumpers.

A DAVID & CHARLES BOOK

A catalogue record for this book is available from the British
Library.

ISBN 0 7153 0136 5

Typeset by ABM Typographics Ltd, Hull
and printed in Great Britain
by Butler & Tanner Ltd, Frome
for David & Charles
Brunel House   Newton Abbot   Devon

CONTENTS

INTRODUCTION

Years ago when my children were small and I, like many other mothers, just knitted little items like bootees, socks and bonnets, I never thought that one day I would write a book about picture knitting. My experience of knitting all that time ago would be to go to a shop, find a suitable pattern, buy the wool and reproduce an exact replica of a garment knitted by the many other purchasers of that same pattern. As I was not at the time a very competent knitter, I considered this to be the only way that knitting could be done. It was only much later when I was deciding to investigate a different approach to the subject, that I realised that it might be possible to knit garments using my own designs. In fact, I achieved this very successfully using the method laid out in this book.

Having purchased graph paper and pencil, I took my first tentative steps at designing my own garments and, to my surprise, it worked – well, almost. Some fine-tuning had to take place, but the end result was a resounding success. My first venture, in the form of a bus design, was accepted by a leading women's magazine and presented as a centrefold. That original bus design is now used as my company's logo.

Getting bolder and gaining confidence with every design, I found that there was hardly any shape that could not be reproduced. Having spent many years designing and making appliqué motifs for jackets, prior to these early tentative steps into knitting, I felt that the process of reproducing figures for knitting was not that dissimilar.

. . . .

Hatfield House and Cawdor Castle with its ghosts show how architecture, including your house or home, can make a very effective design. Cawdor Castle appears courtesy of Countess Cawdor.

The next step was to progress from designing single motif figures into creating whole pictures, again using only graph paper, but much larger sheets. I found that whole scenes could be painted on to the canvas, represented by the front, back and sleeves of a garment. Although sometimes the subject matter may have a naive look to it, at other times very precise and complicated patterns can be produced, if you are patient enough. A look at the picture of Hatfield House on Craft Fair Day (page 6) emphasises this point very well.

There must be many knitters who wish to become designers, yet do not know where to begin, knitters who want to try something a little different and knitters who value a garment that is unique, so it is at them that this book is aimed. I know that there is a demand for picture knitting – almost every day I am asked to create designs for subjects such as a pheasant in heather for a huntsman, a tennis scene for Wimbledon, or a fishing lake or river for a fishing enthusiast. All of these and many more are well within anyone's capabilities and this book shows how to produce picture knitted garments in easy stages.

For those who do not knit, do not be discouraged! Chapter 1 teaches the beginner how to go about it. Nothing is complicated. The type of knitting shown is the most simplistic and basic and, once learned, the beginner can move on confidently to knitting picture jumpers. Chapter 2 takes a step-by-step approach on how to create a graph and how to turn this graph into a garment of your choice.

Glossaries in the book, including the Picture Library at the rear, offer the reader a wealth of choice in subjects. These include people, animals, buildings and many others that will enable designs to be created just with the use of pencil and paper.

1
BACK TO BASICS

I chose the title of this chapter because I hoped that the word 'basic' would attract those people who had never before handled a pair of needles or battled frustratedly with tangled balls of wool, while, at the same time, would offer something to people who do knit. It is, of course, possible that even the most experienced knitters will pick up a hint or two. During the process of researching this chapter I heard the comment 'how simple' on numerous occasions, justifying the inclusion of various techniques.

When book browsing, it is often the book's cover and subject that first attract a potential reader, so, having picked up this book, the desire to knit a picture jumper of your own design may become an interesting and tempting idea and it would be frustrating for this wish to be denied simply because you cannot knit. For many knitters, knitting holds a fascination that makes it become a life-long hobby and friend. To begin to achieve this, knitting has to be learnt easily and it must be fun to do – and knitting picture jumpers certainly is fun! This chapter therefore deals with the simple rudiments of knitting, moving, by easy stages, from casting on through all the elements necessary to equip a non-knitter with sufficient skills to knit his or her own picture garments. Then not only picture garments can be knitted but all types of projects can be undertaken, increasing the knitter's experience.

Knitting is an immense subject where the learning never really stops and this can prove to be both daunting and mystifying to non-knitters. They can often be deterred by their first sight of a complicated pattern written in abbreviations that they do not understand. This chapter aims to dispel these apprehensions. One of the most important aspects of learning is encouragement, as encouragement breeds confidence and confidence makes for easier learning.

The simple and easy-to-read instructions are accompanied by clear sketches that fully illustrate and assist the learning process. Where an instruction has a greater degree of difficulty, two and sometimes three illustrations are included. All of this is laid out in a step-by-step, easy-to-follow format, that, while supplying the beginner with a sufficient knowledge of how to knit, will not confound or confuse by offering the many alternatives available. For example, where there are several methods for increasing and decreasing, those given are either the most simplistic or alternatively are relevant only to the theme of picture knitting, thereby hastening the speed of learning. There is no doubt that when you are learning to knit, advice may be sought (and very often is offered) from experienced knitters. Although experienced knitters are only too pleased to help beginners, beware of too much conflicting advice which may cause confusion.

One of the best pieces of advice to a beginner who is first learning to knit concerns the importance of patience and practice, especially practice. The time you spend practising every technique before you move on to the next stage will reward you when you come to knit your first garment. To put this theory to the test, a simple project to make a knitted hat has been included after the final instructions in this Chapter. It incorporates most of the lessons learnt. The hat matches the design of the racing car featured on the jumper in Chapter 2. In making the hat, all you are required to do is follow an easy pattern and knit pictures in the form of words from a simple graph. This project enables the beginner to make the transition from learning to knitting, in the proper sense, with a completed garment as proof of this achievement.

CASTING ON

Two of the most commonly used methods for casting on are the 'thumb' method that uses one needle with the thumb acting as the second needle, and the 'cable' method that requires the use of two needles. Both methods are effective and very easy to learn. Although the thumb method is suitable for most types of knitting, the cable method may be preferred when you require a firmer edge or when extra stitches are needed at some point in a pattern.

When learning either technique, do not cast on too many or too few stitches. Thirty is about the right number as too many stitches are difficult to handle and too few can give an uneven finish. Also, thirty is a good number with which to proceed on to the next instruction.

Casting on with two needles, a more advanced technique and specifically used for making buttonholes, is described on page 16.

THUMB METHOD

1 Make slip knot approximately 2m (78in) in from end of yarn and place needle through knot. Taking needle into right hand, hold main yarn loosely over index finger and through palm, holding needle securely with thumb and second finger.

2 Take yarn's loose end and hold in left palm; make loop around left thumb; insert needle through loop from left to right (Fig 1).

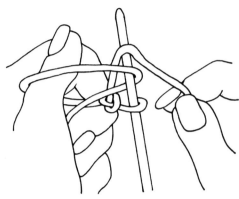

Fig 2

5 Repeat process until the required number of stitches are made. Cut off loose end of yarn, leaving approximately 20cm (8in).

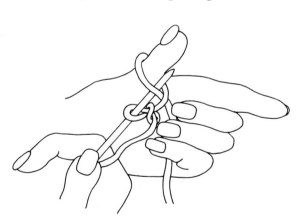

Fig 1

3 Now holding needle with left thumb and index finger and using main yarn, make loop around point of needle, going under and back between tips of finger and thumb (Fig 2).

4 Keeping yarn taut and holding needle with right thumb and index finger, slip left thumb loop over point of needle and pull ends of yarn tight (Fig 3).

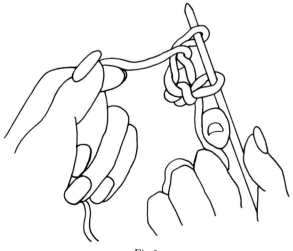

Fig 3

CABLE METHOD

1 Make slip knot about 20cm (8in) from end of yarn and place on left-hand needle. Take second needle into right hand and, holding yarn over index finger and through palm, insert point of needle through loop on left-hand needle from left to right, making sure needle two passes under needle one (Fig 4).

2 With yarn held over right index finger, pass yarn under bottom needle and pull firmly to settle against stitch between both needles (Fig 5).

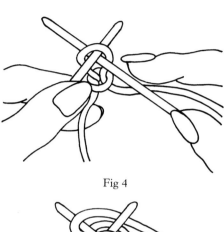

Fig 4

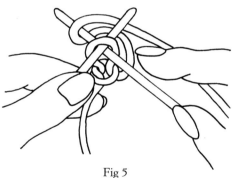

Fig 5

3 Drawing back bottom needle, gather this loop while raising bottom needle to top position (you now have one loop on each needle). Slip loop on right-hand needle on to left-hand needle, pulling yarn tight to form a new stitch of similar size to the first.

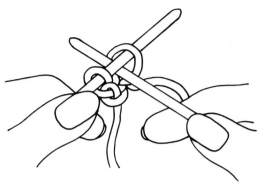

Fig 6

4 Now insert point of right-hand needle between two stitches on left-hand needle instead of through the loop (Fig 6), pass yarn under and round bottom needle and pull to settle between both needles. Continue as in step 3 to form third stitch.

5 Continue as for third stitch until the required number of stitches are made.

HANDY HINT

Inserting the needle between the two stitches *before* tightening the previous loop makes for easier passage of the needle.

KNIT STITCH (K)

Having cleared the first hurdle of casting on, it is now time to commence knitting in the proper sense, starting with the knit stitch (k). This is the first step to be taken towards increasing the knitting on your needles and decreasing the ball of wool in your hand.

In its simplest term, knitting is a clever method of stringing together yarn, twine or string in a series of knots that will not unravel. These knots

or stitches range from simple and basic to decorative and complicated and how they are used eventually forms a creative garment.

'Elephant', using the crew neck with rib bottom pattern (pages 43 or 60), shows an all round picture of elephants on the body and sleeves and is framed top and bottom with a border pattern from the Picture Library.

1 Take needle holding cast-on stitches, into left hand and hold securely across palm with point protruding between thumb and index finger.

2 Taking second needle in right hand, insert through first loop (stitch), making sure that needle two passes under needle one. With yarn at back of knitting and held loosely over right index finger, pass yarn under bottom needle and pull firmly to settle against stitch between both needles (Fig 7).

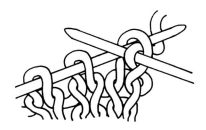

Fig 8

4 Continue this process until all stitches are transferred from needle one to needle two. Then swop the needle holding the knitting from right hand to left hand and you are ready to continue (Fig 9). Consecutive rows of knit stitch are termed garter stitch.

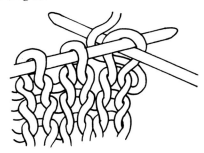

Fig 7

3 Drawing back bottom needle, gather this loop while raising bottom needle to top position. Slip loop off left-hand needle, thereby making a knit stitch (Fig 8).

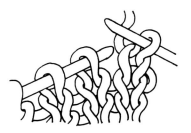

Fig 9

PURL STITCH (P)

From knit stitch we now move to purl (p), which, when combined with knit is termed stocking stitch and forms the basis for the majority of knitting in this book. After completing a few rows of both knit and purl you will begin to see a build-up of knitting. Do not worry about feeling clumsy or slow as this will soon change as experience is gained. As progress is made it is well worth considering the importance of consistent tension. Everyone knits differently – some tightly, some loosely. No matter how you knit, try not to vary your tension. One or the other is acceptable as any problems arising from this can be rectified by a change of needle size. This is discussed along with other tension-related problems later in the chapter.

1 Keeping needle containing stitches in left hand and yarn at front of knitting, place right-hand needle through first loop from right to left (Fig 10), this time making sure that right-hand needle is in the top position.

2 Loop yarn around right-hand needle (Fig 11) and pull firmly to settle against stitch between

Fig 10

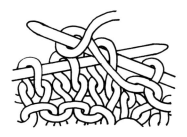

Fig 11

3 Continue this process until all stitches are transferred from needle one to needle two. Then change knitting from right hand to left hand and you are ready to continue.

needles. Drawing back top needle, gather this loop while lowering top needle to bottom position (Fig 12). Slip loop off left-hand needle and gently tighten, thereby making a purl stitch.

Fig 12

STOCKING STITCH (ST ST)

Having completed a few rows of knit and purl, what is now required is as much practice as possible. To achieve this, continue knitting in stocking stitch until you have used up the ball of yarn that you started with. This will help your fingers to become flexible and tension to improve.

Stocking stitch starts with row 1 (right side) knit (Fig 13), followed by row 2 (wrong side) purl (Fig 14), and repeats in this manner for as long as required. It is the most common stitch in knitting and forms the basis of most simple garments and very often the background when more complicated patterns are required. When creating picture jumpers it is the perfect stitch and is used throughout this book.

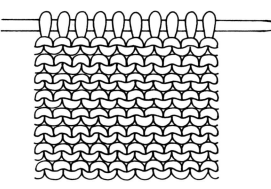

Fig 14

HANDY HINT

The wrong side of stocking stitch is known as reverse stocking stitch and can be used on the right side of garments to give additional flair to patterns in such shapes as raised diamonds, triangles, and so on.

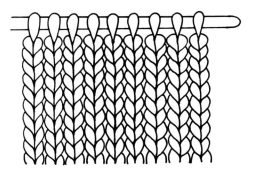

Fig 13

· 13 ·

SINGLE RIB (RIB)

Rib is used mainly to knit the neck, cuffs and bottoms of garments to give them a traditional shape; usually ribs are the only parts that fit snugly to the body, keeping you warm on winter days. A well-knitted rib using quality yarn has tremendous elasticity that will last for years, no matter how often the garment is washed or worn. A good jumper with loose cuffs, wobbly neck and saggy bottom is not a pretty sight (Fig 15).

Rib is easiest when knitted using an even number of stitches, so be aware of this when knitting rib from the start of a garment. However, the exception is when you knit front cardigan bands that require buttonholes. These are better achieved by using an odd number of stitches so that the hole falls central to the band (see page 16).

The simple rib used throughout this book is made of one stitch knit, then one stitch purl, followed by one stitch knit and so on, until the required number of rows are completed or a certain length achieved. This produces the ladder effect shown in Fig 15 and you will see that the pattern is identical on both the front and the back of the garment.

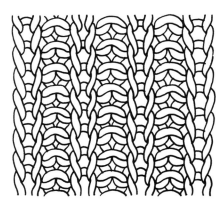

Fig 15

INCREASING (INC)

Increasing the width of a garment is often necessary – for example, sleeves are not the same size at the wrist as they are at the shoulder, and in order to achieve this shaped effect, more stitches need to be added. This then becomes an important feature in the final shape and fit of the garment.

Both knit and purl rows are suitable for increasing. If your pattern calls for extra stitches on every fifth row, then a first row knit increase will be followed by a sixth row purl increase and so on. A useful tip is to work the first stitch in the row as normal, before increasing. This helps to achieve a neat finish. Practise well before using!

To increase on a knit row: knit into the front of the stitch, gather but do not slip loop off needle (Fig 16), then knit into the back of the same stitch, gather, then slip loop from left needle to right.

To increase on a purl row: purl into the front of the stitch, gather but do not slip loop off needle, then purl into the back of the same stitch, gather and slip loop from left to right needle. In both instances you will find that your one stitch has become two (Fig 17).

Fig 16

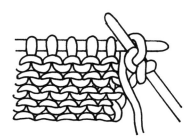

Fig 17

DECREASING (DEC)

Decreasing is used to shape your garment – especially, for example, around necklines – and is a very simple procedure in comparison to increasing.

When a pattern calls for decreasing by one stitch only, use one of the following methods. If you need to decrease by more than one stitch at a time, refer to 'casting off' below.

1 Knit two together (k2 tog)
Insert point of needle through two stitches at the same time and work as one.

2 Pass slipped stitch over (psso)
Slip first loop from left to right needle, take following loop and knit a stitch. Using left needle, pass first loop back over knitted stitch and drop off needle.

CASTING OFF

Casting off is the method used to finish off and complete a piece of knitting or when a decrease of more than one stitch at a time is required, as in shoulder shaping. Either knit or purl may be used for casting off. When casting off in rib, especially where maximum elasticity is of prime importance, such as on neckbands remember to cast off using rib stitch. Where stocking stitch has been used, cast off in either knit or purl according to which is appropriate. It is important to avoid casting off too tightly, and if this is a problem, compensate for it by changing the right-hand needle for one that is one size larger for the final cast-off row.

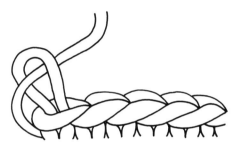

Fig 19

Slip the first loop from left to right needle, then take the following loop and knit a stitch. Now using your left needle, pass the first loop back over the knitted stitch (Fig 18) and drop it off the needle. You are now left with the knitted stitch on the right-hand needle. Treating this as your first loop, repeat the process. Continue until the required number of stitches have been cast off. When casting off all the stitches, cast off in the method described until only one stitch remains on the right-hand needle (Fig 19) and cut off yarn leaving approximately 30cm (12in). Pull stitch to make a larger loop, remove needle, pass cut end of yarn through loop and pull tight, thus forming a secure knot.

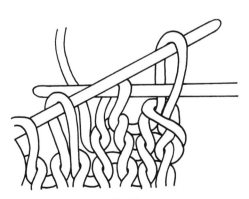

Fig 18

TENSION

Tension is the most problematic and most difficult technique to achieve consistently. Factors include tight or loose knitters, needle size, yarn quality and yarn thickness. Poor quality yarn can contribute to incorrect tension as it is more likely to vary in thickness and weight. Colours affect tension too – the darker the dye, the thicker the wool. All these factors can combine to play havoc with sizing.

To try to achieve the required dimensions and to limit the problems, knit tension squares whenever a change of yarn or pattern takes place.

To obtain the correct tension as stated in the pattern, knit a square of no less than 12cm (5in). This is bigger than necessary but will ensure when the square is measured that the tension is not affected by the edges, which may be slightly tighter than the centre.

If, after measuring the square, you find too many stitches, use larger needles; conversely, if you have too few stitches, use smaller needles. Continue to do this until the correct tension is achieved (Fig 20).

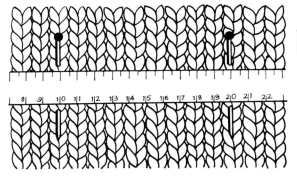

Fig 20

ADVANCED TECHNIQUES

MAKING A BUTTONHOLE

The example of a buttonhole featured here uses seven stitches of rib. This enables the finished hole to be central and, when viewed buttoned up, will centralise the button to the band.

All stitches surrounding the hole must be worked as firmly and as tightly as possible to ensure long-lasting wear. If you find after knitting that the buttonhole is on the loose side, rectify this by darning several strands of yarn around the opening. This will help to close down and tighten the hole at the same time. It is easier to reduce too large a buttonhole than to try to squeeze large buttons through small holes.

The making of buttonholes requires casting on using the two-needle method as follows:

Cast on using the cable method (page 10) but work all the stitches as for the second stitch and not by inserting the needle between the stitches as in the third stitch.

1 Arriving at the required position of the buttonhole, work 2 stitches in rib, cast off 3 stitches and finish row in rib.

2 On the next row, work 2 stitches in rib, then swop the needles to other hands, cast on 3 stitches as described above, replacing all stitches cast off in previous row, swop needles again and work remaining stitches (Fig 21).

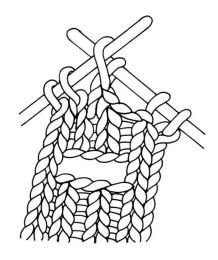

Fig 21

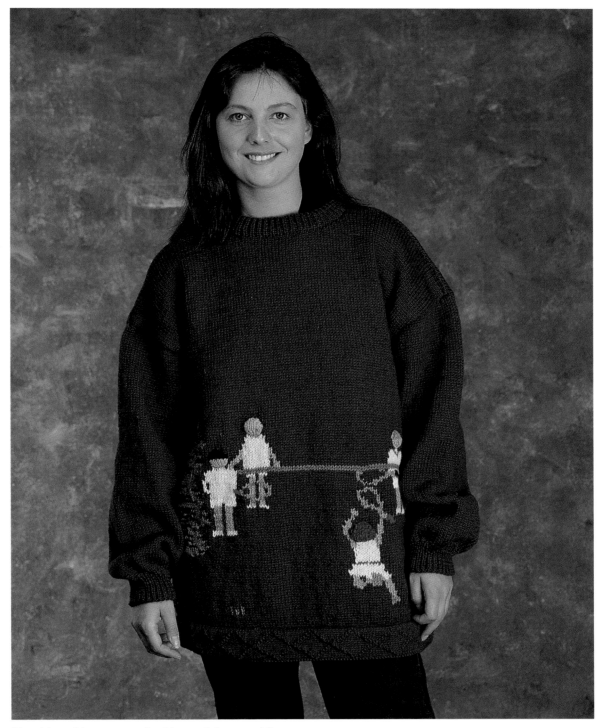

'Tennis' combines crew neck with a tunic bottom. After completing the hem, continue as for the crew neck pattern. Use the Picture Library and Countryside theme for the people and trees.

MAKING A HEM

Knitting stitches together from two separate rows is a technique used in this book solely for hem making. It is featured in the basic pattern for the roll neck with tunic bottom (page 62) and therefore shows its use in the simplest form.

1 Using a third needle, pick up cast-on stitches as shown in Fig 22.

2 Bring both needles together, making sure that the wrong side of the knitting is inside. Working both needles as one in the left hand, knit until the third needle is disposed with. This will knit both edges firmly together and complete hem (Fig 23).

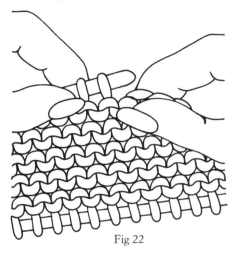

Fig 22

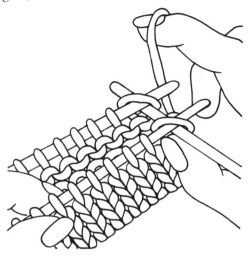

Fig 23

MAKING A POCKET

Pockets take various forms. There are knitted-in pockets, stitched-on patch pockets and pockets purely for decorative use. Decorative pockets are shown here as they are used only to keep in place the varying types of finger puppets and animals that form part of the designs, especially those made for children, although adults seem to like them too.

As it is important that the pockets blend in with the garment, the use of supporting ribs and other techniques is not required.

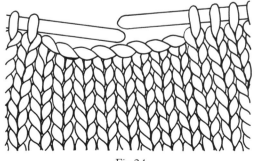

Fig 24

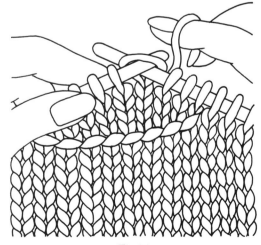

Fig 25

1 Knit a square of stocking stitch to the size of pocket required and leave on a spare needle.
2 Continue knitting garment until you reach the desired pocket position, then cast off the same number of stitches as knitted in the square (Fig 24).
3 On the next row, work until first cast-off stitch is reached, then work in the stitches from the square (Fig 25) until all the stitches have been knitted in and the third needle has been disposed of. Then complete the row as normal and continue until the piece is finished.
4 The pocket sides and bottom are then slip stitched into position to form a small pocket for puppets.

KNITTING WITH TWO OR MORE COLOURS

Picture jumpers, by their very nature, are made up of different colours and because of this, what on the outside appears to be a well-ordered pattern, on the inside can become, if allowed, a mass of tangled ends. To limit this as much as possible, study the pattern and make a list of all the colours required, then, with the exception of the background colour, wind off small balls of each, making an estimate of the amounts needed. Where just a few stitches of a colour are needed, simply cut pieces of yarn to a suitable length, (approximately 1cm (½in) per stitch), taking care to leave a minimum of 15cm (6in) at both ends. Do not carry yarns across the back of the work when changing colours – always bring in separate pieces of yarn as you work. Carrying yarns across will distort the pattern and give a disappointing final result.

When finishing with a colour, simply cut off, leaving 15cm (6in) ready to be sewn in when the whole piece is finished.

When joining in a new colour, start your new colour at least 15cm (6in) in from the end of the yarn and be sure to knit the first stitch in firmly. Failure to do this may cause holes to appear at a later date.

1 To start a new colour, pass right-hand needle through loop and lay new colour over the right-hand needle and between needle points (Fig 26). Then, working this stitch in the previous colour, as normal, gather both colours at the same time. Continue to knit using your new colour, making sure to pull the yarn firmly and tight. This point is especially important when working cotton which lacks stretch.
2 When arriving at a second colour already knitted in, always cross over both yarns. Failure to do this can result in a 'holey' appearance.

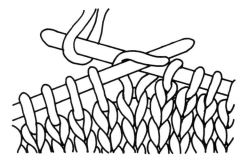

Fig 26

Put right-hand needle through loop of colour to be knitted into and simply cross over the two colours before continuing further, then knit as normal. When knitting stripes, take yarns loosely up sides of work until needed. This avoids needless darning in.

The jumper worn by Hannah in 'Jungle theme', page 107, is here reversed showing all loose ends finished off.

FINISHING

Having completed the knitting of a front, back and two sleeves, you now need to assemble them into a completed garment, ready to wear. This is one of the most important tasks and it needs to be carried out with patience and precision.

Neatly and firmly sewing the pieces together in line ensures that the garment will remain in one piece long after holes appear in the elbows. Any amount of extra time spent on this important task greatly benefits the final outcome.

■ ■

'Elephant' shows the vibrancy of gold thread and chenille when used with plain or rather dull yarns.

TYING IN

Before commencing seam finishing, the tying in or sewing in of all loose ends must be carried out. Using a blunt-ended darning needle, carefully darn these into their own colour, criss-crossing each one where possible. Where only one stitch has been knitted, each end can be tied securely to its nearest neighbour, thereby eliminating the need to darn into a different colour. After all ends are tied in, trim any surplus yarn.

SEAM FINISHING

When seam finishing, be sure to use the same coloured yarn as that of the section being sewn.

This will almost certainly mean that you will need to use several different colours as each pattern or design is met. A blunt-ended darning needle is the best tool to use, although if the garment is made of cotton, use a standard darning needle. Of the two methods described below, the most suitable seam finishing is the second method. The design and pattern can be seen at all times, which ensures that across-seam patterns match.

Method 1
Bring the two pieces to be joined right sides together and match row for row across seam. Using back stitch, stitch the two pieces together, taking a very small seam allowance of one or, at the most, two stitches (Fig 27). Sew together, keeping the stitches small and close. This gives a most secure and extremely neat finish.

Method 2
When the garment has a design that crosses from one piece to the other, lay the two edges to be sewn side by side with right side up, matching row for row. This enables the pattern to be seen. Using a blunt-ended darning needle with the correct colour yarn, pick up the loop between the first and second stitch, one stitch in from each side, and pull edges firmly together (Fig 28). Continue in this fashion until all stitches have been picked up and the seam completed.

HANDY HINTS
Try not to use both methods on the same garment unless pattern states otherwise.

Before sewing garment, pin seams together every 8-10cm (3-4in) which will help to stop seams puckering.

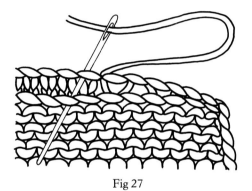

Fig 27

Fig 28

DECORATIVE TECHNIQUES

SWISS DARNING

This stitch can be added to the surface of a garment after its completion and is an excellent way of correcting the odd error that has slipped by unnoticed or to create single dots of colour.

Bring a blunt-ended darning needle and appropriately coloured yarn from the back of the garment to the front at the base of the stitch that needs to be covered. Taking the yarn behind the stitch immediately above, sew through from left to right (Fig 29). Return needle to back at initial point of entry.

Fig 29

Above 'Flower shop' is decorated with swiss-darned leaves and flowers. Use this method where large amounts of single stitches are required.

Opposite Chain stitch is used to outline and highlight details that can become lost or overshadowed in this ABC 123 nursery picture.

CHAIN STITCH OR LAZY DAISY

When this stitch is used correctly it is certain to add interest to a pattern, as its main function, especially in picture knitting, is to heighten effect and outline obscure subjects. Another use is to add details such as strings to kites.

Using the same blunt-ended darning needle with yarn, insert from back to front. When all the yarn is pulled through, leaving sufficient at back to secure, return needle only through same hole and push point of needle to the front, surfacing two or three stitches above needle entry point. Loop the yarn around point of needle, then, drawing needle through loop, pull yarn tight. Return needle slightly above point of completed stitch and secure loop (Fig 30). The use of a single stitch in this manner is most suitable for such items as flower petals, and so on, and as such is worthy of its name 'Lazy Daisy'. To turn it into a chain of several stitches, repeat as for Lazy Daisy but do not return needle for securing until final stitch has been completed.

Fig 30

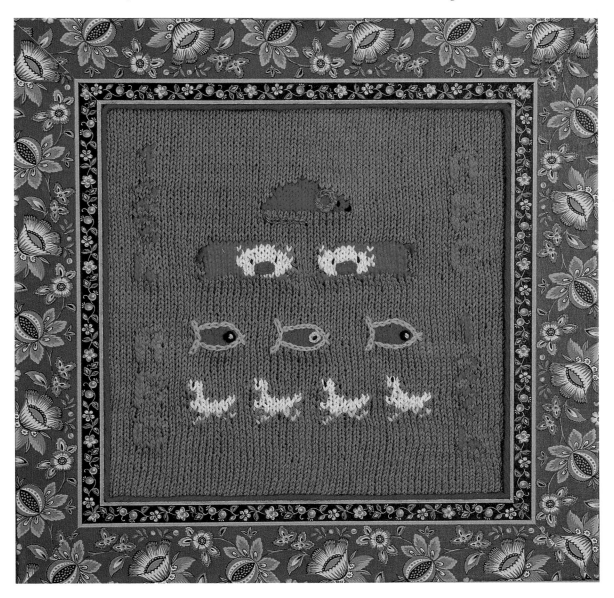

KNITTING WITH FABRIC

While the garment is being made, it is worthwhile bearing in mind the possibilities afforded by the use of knitting with materials other than yarn. One of these possibilities is the use of fabric. To do this, take a suitable and well-patterned cotton lawn that will not fray, cut into very fine strips and knit into the garment as just another yarn. The frequent changes of colour that occur in the knitting of pictures makes its introduction very simple indeed. Such items as a person's dress, curtains to

To obtain interesting textures in the 'cafe' design, knit in floral lawn and ribbon as shown in the dress, umbrella and sun.

windows and sunblinds can be enhanced by its use. Other materials such as gold and silver threads, bouclé yarn, chenille, sequins, beads and ribbons all have a place in the picture jumper. Use your imagination and don't be afraid to experiment.

Hat

This simple hat has a hat-band (Fig 31) using basic stitches and two or more colours. Its making pulls together all your new skills.

The hat uses many of the basic knitting methods, and is shown in a size suitable for most children. As everything learned so far is only a means to better things, it is well worth taking care on it, as the pattern includes most of the skills necessary for picture knitting.

If the hat is for an adult, add extra stitches equally to each side of the graph and more rows, if required, to its length. When working from a graph, be sure to work all knit (k) rows from right to left and all purl (p) rows from left to right.

MAKING UP

Be sure to sew in all loose yarn ends and remove surplus yarn prior to picking up cast-on stitches to commence hem. Although the loose ends will not be seen after the hem is completed, it is well worth taking the time to do this to ensure a long-lasting and neat finish. Sew up the hat as described in the seam finishing instructions on pages 20–1, using method 2 for the sides, as this enables you to match the pattern perfectly, and method 1 for completing the top.

When the hat is finished, push in corners to give shape and make a finger puppet for the pocket (see finger puppet instructions, pages 66–8).

Fig 31

Aran weight wool 4½mm and 3¾mm needles			
Tension	21sts, 26 rows to 10cm in st st, using 4½mm needles		
Size	44cm (17in) around head, 20cm (8in) long		
START OF PATTERN			
Using red, cast on with 3¾mm needles		Stitches	111
Work in st st starting with k row for		Rows	15
Work 1 row knit			
Change to black and begin working from chart, starting with k row			
	14th row of chart (p) work	Stitches	78
	Cast off for pocket (dotted line in Fig 31)	Stitches	8
Hem and pocket	Continue in p to end of row		
	Sew in loose yarn ends before commencing next row		
	Next row (last row of chart) knit in hem (see Making a Hem, page 18)		
	(When the 8 cast-off stitches are reached, knit stitches from casting-on row only, as the previously cast-off stitches will form pocket opening)		
Crown	Using black, change to 4½mm needles and work in st st	Rows	44
	Cast off		
See making up instructions above			

2
DESIGN AND BUILD

Before you start to knit a garment that is to feature the design of your choice, especially the overall picture variety that forms the basis of this book, you will probably need some help and guidance on the techniques. This chapter therefore discusses and offers advice on what are the most suitable tools to use for writing, drawing, and so on. Advice on graph paper, adding colour, and the use of photocopies is mentioned to give the reader or the potential designer an insight into their uses. For instance, when you come to make your own working graph, you will understand immediately why these items are necessary.

When selecting a subject from which to create a design, it is easy to be spoilt for choice, unless, of course, the choice is obvious. For example, designing a garment around a fishing scene for a fishing enthusiast would present no problem of choice at all. In fact, the majority of your designs will be selected in this way. To show one method of design selection, I have taken a picture of a

Formula One race-track meeting and from this have reproduced on graph paper the items required to design a very colourful and topical garment, based on motor-racing. This is followed by a number of possible designs depicting the same theme, using a variety of colourways. One of these designs is then carried through to completion showing graphs for front, back and sleeves, complete with full instructions.

When embarking upon creating designs, either for yourself or for a member of your family, feel free to let your imagination run riot, at least to begin with. Any mad extravagances will be curtailed at a later stage, especially when you are faced with the task of fitting it all on to one garment. When I am looking for inspiration for new designs, I try to have with me what I call loosely my designer kit, consisting of pencil and pad, camera, photographic memory and so on, although more often than not when I do have inspiration, my designer's kit is nowhere to be found! As a consequence, many of my designs have to be translated from scraps of paper. This is a problem for all those who are constantly in need of inspiration for new designs.

When you are looking for inspiration, search through children's books, old photographs, newspapers, or consider themes such as Christmas, sport, the big outdoors – the list is endless. For most people who do not knit as a business but who knit solely for family and pleasure, an idea for a design will often project itself immediately, especially when knitting is a labour of love for children or grand-children. It may be that the person for whom the garment is being made plays

Left The motor-racing scene that provided the inspiration for the finished jumper, hat and socks (*right*).

football, cricket or tennis; they may swim, wind-surf or sail, ride horses, go racing, climb mountains or even deep-sea dive – anything in fact, from anchor throwing to zebra-riding! All of these subjects and many more with a little thought and some help, can find their way on to an eye-catching and unique garment. When wishing to build on a deisgn to increase its attraction or high-light its theme, do not hesitate to decorate or sur-round the central idea with its associated trivia. If, for example, the central theme is horse-riding, then use such symbols as horse-shoes, riding whips, rosettes and stirrups. Either scattered about haphazardly or used in an orderly fashion for hems, ribs or sleeve cuffs, such details enhance considerably any picture jumper.

Where knitting techniques are concerned, I have made a conscious effort to keep to the simple and basic; no complicated or intricate knitting is called for that will confuse anyone who has perse-vered through Chapter 1 and who may have only rudimentary skills.

Although in this chapter only one specific de-sign is used as a guide, later in the book simple basic patterns are included that can be used for the creation of your own designs. Using these patterns, combined with selected items from the Picture Library, will enable picture jumper de-signs to be built up to suit any requirements. In this way you will be on the road to gaining greater experience, which will finally lead you to create inspired designs from your own imagination.

I cannot express strongly enough just how much pleasure there is to be obtained from this form of knitting. Watching the designs begin to appear as you knit creates the urge to knit faster, especially when the design first drawn on paper begins to take on the shape you intend. This then becomes a tremendous boost to your confidence and before you know it another jumper is on its way.

MATERIALS AND THEIR USES

Strictly speaking, all that is needed to design a picture garment is a pencil and some graph paper. However, designs created on scraps of paper can have their shortcomings and therefore need to be transferred to something more substantial. Furthermore, the design may finally end up as part of your knitting pattern library to be called

upon at a later date, or to pass on to an admirer who desires a garment of the same design. With this in mind, do spend some time on the subject. Although an idea can be inspired and come to mind in a flash, transforming that idea into a finished pattern usually takes longer.

Probably the most worrying aspect of design-ing is a person's inability to draw or sketch in a lifelike or proportionate way. Although art train-ing is desirable, it is not essential. What removes anxiety in this quarter is the wonderful use to which tracing paper and graph paper can be put. These items certainly ease the burden of drawing and sketching and make life easy for everyone. So, with the intention to make and keep a well-finished design for future use, it is worth learning some of the tricks and rules used by many full-time or professional designers. Most of these rules and tricks are simply common sense, but all are worthy of a mention.

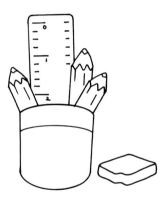

Fig 1

Soft leaded but very sharp pencils are essential (Fig 1). Alternatively, for rough sketches and final outlines a propelling pencil with 0.5mm leads re-moves the need for constant sharpening. The use of soft leads in either case enables all traces to be removed on completion and for this a good quality eraser is a must. Many so called erasers are just blocks of plastic and are not *true* erasers; con-sequently, they often do not rub out cleanly while at the same time they damage the paper's surface. This in turn causes the ink to penetrate the paper, leaving an uneven edge to the finished outline. In the search for a suitable pen, do not be tempted to use a ball-point pen. Find an illustrator's pen that is not too fine; around 0.04 or 0.05 is the best as this size leaves a bold and clearly defined edge. This outline becomes a very useful aid when you are reading the graph and knitting at the same time and makes life easier when you colour in the finished graph. Be sure that the pen you choose contains permanent ink. Many pens contain inks that cause problems by running when they come into contact with water-based colourings such as felt pens. Test them out before you buy one by taking a felt pen with you, preferably a light coloured one, and going over the ink when dry to prove that it does not smudge.

When you have found a suitable subject for a design, you may then feel unable either to sketch or to draw it sufficiently well. The use of tracing paper is the answer. After tracing the subject, transfer the outline to graph paper before 'contouring' or 'squaring up' as described on pages 30–1. Apart from transferring a design from one place to another, tracing paper can be used to give a mirror image of itself. A person traced walking from left to right can be reversed to become a person walking from right to left.

Graph paper is available in a large variety of sizes. These sizes vary in the size of squares and the size of sheets upon which the squares are printed, and as a result you may be confused about which size to choose. In fact, any and all sizes of graph paper are suitable; just remember that one square is equal to one stitch. The most common graph paper to use is 2/10/20mm which can be purchased from most shops dealing in writing materials and stationery and it comes in pads of A4 size. This is the size of graph paper that is used throughout this book (Fig 2). Graph paper with larger squares is available for anyone who might need something a little clearer. Provided that the same number of squares are used in each case, the outcome will remain the same and both sizes are suitable for photocopying. It is possible to purchase graph paper that gives an elongated effect because it has more squares from top to bottom than it has from side to side over the same area. Unfortunately, this paper is not easily obtainable and it is not likely to be stocked by the average high street stationers.

Having inked in the outline of the subjects that form the completed design, using a ruler with an ink edge to avoid smudging, it is well worth taking the time to colour in the design to give an impres-

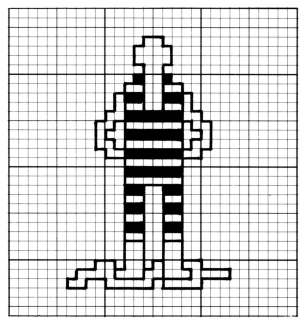

Fig 2

sion of how it will look when knitted. Colouring can be done using crayons, chalks, felt pens or whatever suits you. Probably the cheapest and most commonly used are felt pens, mainly because of the large choice of colours available. However, felt pens used on a normal paper surface tend to bleed into the paper, giving an uneven and blotchy finish. To prevent this happening, have the design colour photocopied and then colour in the photocopy. The surface that the paper obtains by this process will eliminate the problem. Also on the market, but available only from good art shops, are non-bleed pens with brushes at one end and normal tips at the other, but even when these pens are used, it is still recommended that you photocopy first. A further advantage of using a photocopy is that a number of copies may be taken and used to show various colour combinations before you decide which yarns to purchase for the final garment.

BUILDING A DESIGN FROM A SELECTED SUBJECT

The photograph on page 26 shows a typical Formula One meeting on race day, exhibiting all the colour and excitement that is associated with the sport. The only items missing from this scene are the smell and the noise. What it does contain, however, is the bustle of people, the cars and their drivers, sponsors' logos, numbers and the chequered flag, and it is these items that make it such an ideal subject for demonstrating a picture jumper design.

Using the body section as the track, racing cars can be positioned anywhere and everywhere and, provided they all face the same direction, they will give a suitable impression of racing. Having people behind barriers looking on helps to heighten this effect, while at the same time stationary cars on sleeves can be vehicles in pits awaiting attention or refuelling. If all this hubbub is surrounded with logos, a selection of numbers and chequered flags, you can finish up with a very exciting product, provided, of course, that all the details are brought together in a carefully balanced design.

The jumpers on page 27 show very clearly how different designs on the same subject may vary, especially as I have taken the liberty either to add or omit various items to emphasise the point. Shortage of space does not allow for all possible alternatives.

The first option shows cars racing and spectators behind barriers, knitted in a black colourway. Option number two combines all this with liberal use of the chequered flag motif and both the drivers' and sponsors' logos but on a red background. The impression gained at this point is that option one is too sparse and fails to capture the image sufficiently and option two is overdone. So option three becomes a suitable halfway house that I feel fully captures the atmosphere of the track, the smell of the oil and so on, and as such would be very happily worn by any fan of motor-racing. This then becomes the final design, as shown on page 32, with a choice of colourways.

MAKING A WORKING GRAPH

A working graph is the method used to convert a sketch, drawing or tracing of a person or object on to a graph, from which can be knitted an almost exact facsimile. Each square of the graph, within the figure, stretching from side to side or from top to toe represents one knitted stitch. Where the natural breaks occur, such as head, body and trousers, these will form most changes of colour.

The use of 'man with wheelbarrow' to demonstrate this is particularly appropriate in a chapter called 'Design and Build'. He shows not only how to change from sketch to graph but he also embodies almost all the ingredients to make successful picture jumpers. It can be seen that not only people can be transposed but so can objects of irregular and regular form, such as those seen in the wheelbarrow. Furthermore, as all good designs should have moving as well as static features, the man is a good example of how to create an impression of motion.

Whatever form a design takes, it is most likely that suitable subjects, once found, will then need to be copied on to graph paper to be reproduced on to your jumper pattern. Fig 3 shows a simple sketch ready for contouring or squaring up. Once you have made the sketch you may like to experiment with colour combinations (Fig 4) before transferring the outline of the drawing on to the nearest possible graph line of the paper (Fig 5). Be sure to use a soft pencil for sketching and an illustrator pen for the graph line. When complete, a simple erasing of the pencil line leaves a bold outline. A knitted piece 20 stitches wide by 20 rows long does not knit a square as you might think. What does happen is that the piece knits up considerably wider than it is long, so, when you have transferred the sketch on to graph paper, slightly elongate the shape to counteract this problem (Fig 6). The general rule of thumb is that the item should be slightly thinner and longer than normal, and this must be taken into consideration when drawing sketches. For example, a wheel that is 5 squares high and 5 squares wide must be reduced by one square in width or the impression will be a wheel with a flat tyre! A glance at the Picture Library in Chapter 8 will give a good idea of how many squares you should have in both height and width. Should there by any doubt about this, I recommend knitting the item in question before you incorporate it into your design, adjustments can be made at this point. It is here that the specialised elongated graph paper comes into its own, although I must admit that I have never found it necessary. The small adjustments required to obtain correct proportions are so easy and come naturally after a short while.

Finish squaring off and begin to add the colour (Fig 7). Aim for a result that will knit up to look as realistic as possible (Fig 8).

Fig 3   A simple sketch ready for contouring or squaring up

Fig 4   Decide on your colours

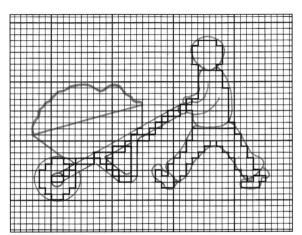

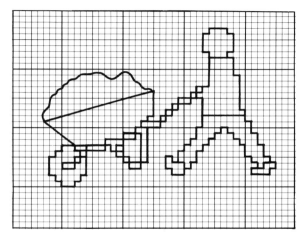

Fig 5   Transfer it onto graph paper using a soft pencil, then follow the nearest graph line with a fine pen

Fig 6   The shape is elongated to compensate

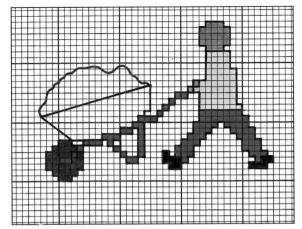

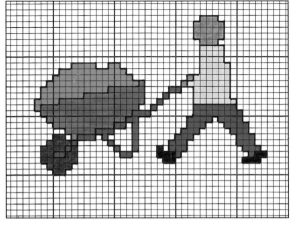

Fig 7   Add the colour and adjust as necessary

Fig 8   The finished design follows the lines of the graph paper while remaining as realistic as possible

INSTRUCTIONS FOR JUMPER

The graphs depicting the motor-racing scene are shown in the three smallest sizes using the basic pattern crew neck with rib bottom as shown in Chapter 3 (pages 43–4). The racing car on the front incorporates a pocket for a finger puppet driver (see page 18 for instructions to make the pocket). Instructions for finger puppets and knitted heads are shown on pages 66–8. As the subject has a wide appeal, there is no reason why this should not be extended to suit adults as well. To do this, simply make up a new pattern by using sheets of graph paper of a size large enough to take into account the number of stitches required, remembering that one stitch of knitting is equal to one square of graph. Using any of the three basic patterns shown in Chapter 3, select whichever adult size is required and draw out a graph to match.

Having decided to make an adult jumper, you will find that the extra space available is a wonderful advantage. Many more features can be added, not only those shown in the racing scene glossary, but the Picture Library may inspire you.

SPECIAL INSTRUCTIONS FOR SMALLEST JUMPER

In order to knit the smallest jumper, some slight alterations are needed. Rather than reduce every detail in an effort to fit it on to so small a garment, simply commence the pattern earlier. Starting with the front, commence knitting the black checks immediately after completing rib, then start the racing car on the fourteenth row of stocking stitch – that is, eight rows fewer than shown on graph. For the back, again start black checks immediately after rib, as with front. Then knit first racing car in normal position as shown on graph. When car is complete, work two rows stocking stitch only and then start second car. This reduces the graph by eight rows to match front. To avoid knitting the wrong size by mistake, it is worthwhile, as well as good practice, to draw a graph of your own to represent this smallest size garment.

■ ■

Left Ben and Christopher wearing final design of motor-racing jumper showing the effect of all round pattern as though on a race track.

MATCHING PATTERNS AND SHAPES

What makes picture knitting different from most other styles of knitwear is its ability to carry a pattern shape or design all around the garment. Most knitwear has patterns that run vertically or horizontally that end either at neck and rib or at side seams. One of the aims of picture knitting is to carry the pattern across these traditional stopping points. It is not difficult to do this, provided a certain amount of care is taken. Using the racing car garment as an example (Fig 9), when carrying over a pattern from front to back or vice versa, be sure that a minimum of two stitches either side of the seam coincide on the same row of both graphs. This ensures perfect matching when sewing up. Do check and even double check when drawing both graphs that all patterns that are intended to cross over do so on the same line of graph. On the racing car jumper the barrier and the overlapping car are sited below the sleeves, allowing for non-interference of pattern flow.

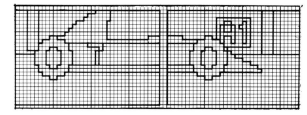

Fig 9

BORDER PATTERNS

When drawing border patterns on your graphs, such as the chequered flag border on the racing jumper (page 32), be sure to commence the pattern from the square that falls centre to the width of your pattern and then work outwards both left and right with the design. Although on some patterns the design will exactly equal the number of stitches available, do not be concerned if it fails to do this, as everything will match sufficiently when seams are sewn together. If the border happens to be of a diamond pattern or similar, finish pattern at the last complete diamond prior to arriving at the seam edge. This will ensure that you do not have to match a partial or incomplete pattern. Paying attention to finishing details such as continuous borders makes a huge difference in quality, and never fails to impress.

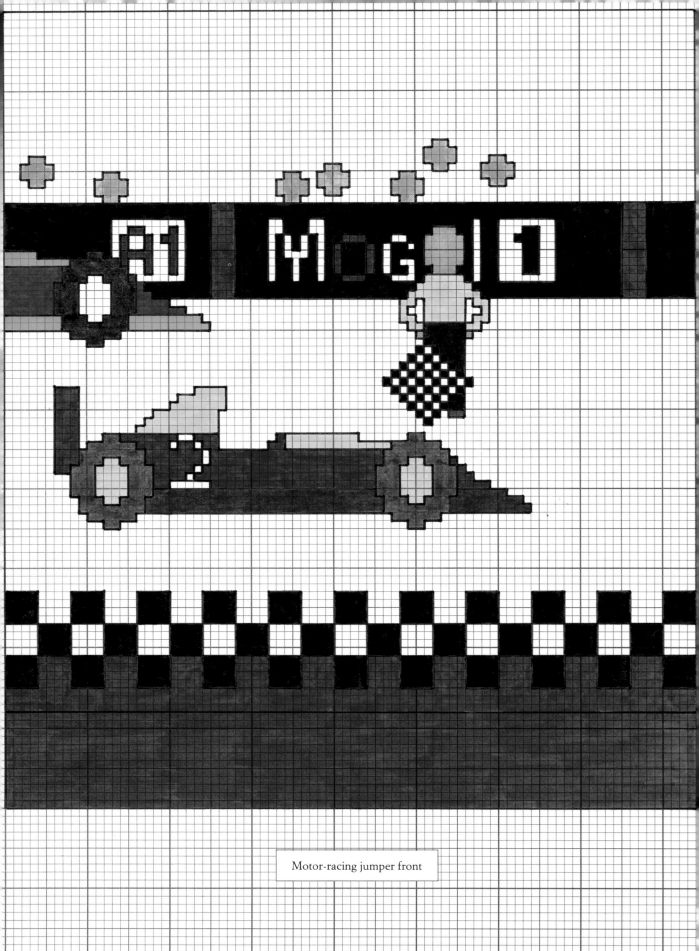

Motor-racing jumper front

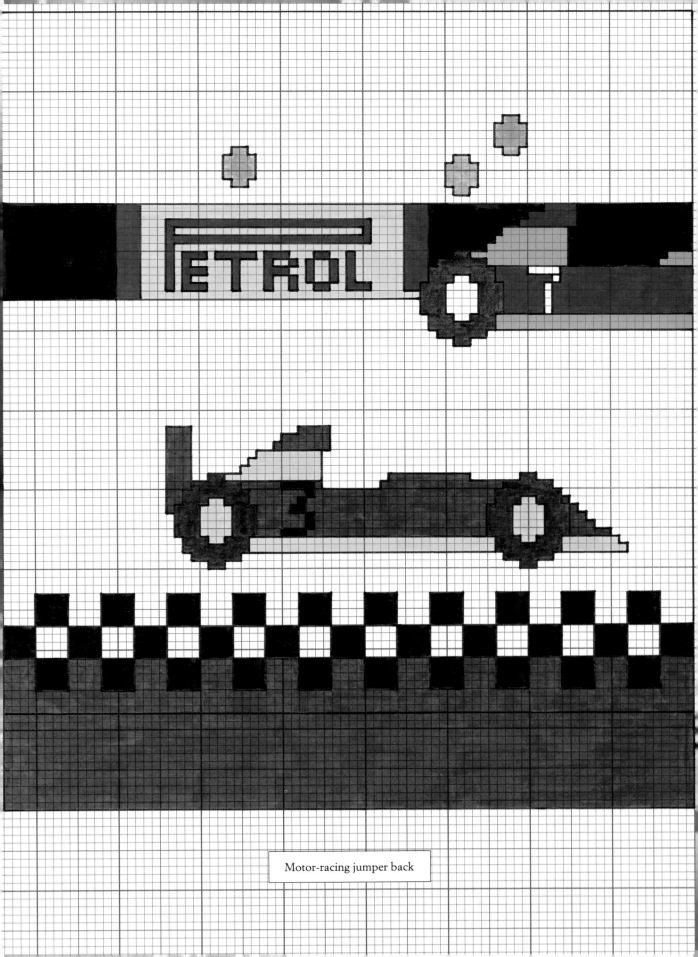

Motor-racing jumper back

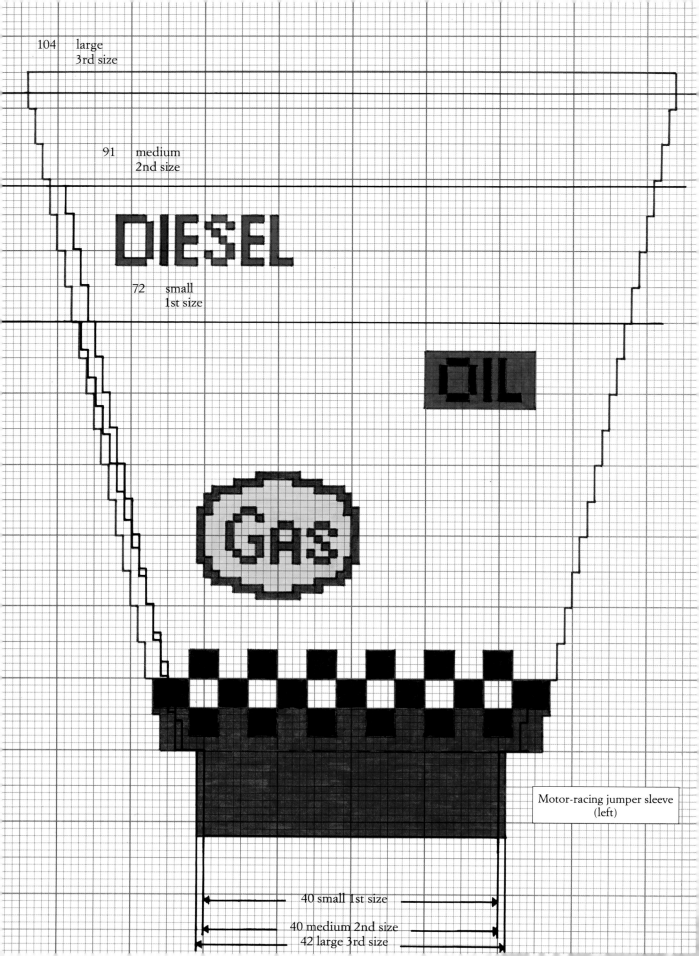

104   large
3rd size

91   medium
2nd size

DIESEL

72   small
1st size

OIL

GAS

Motor-racing jumper sleeve
(left)

40 small 1st size

40 medium 2nd size

42 large 3rd size

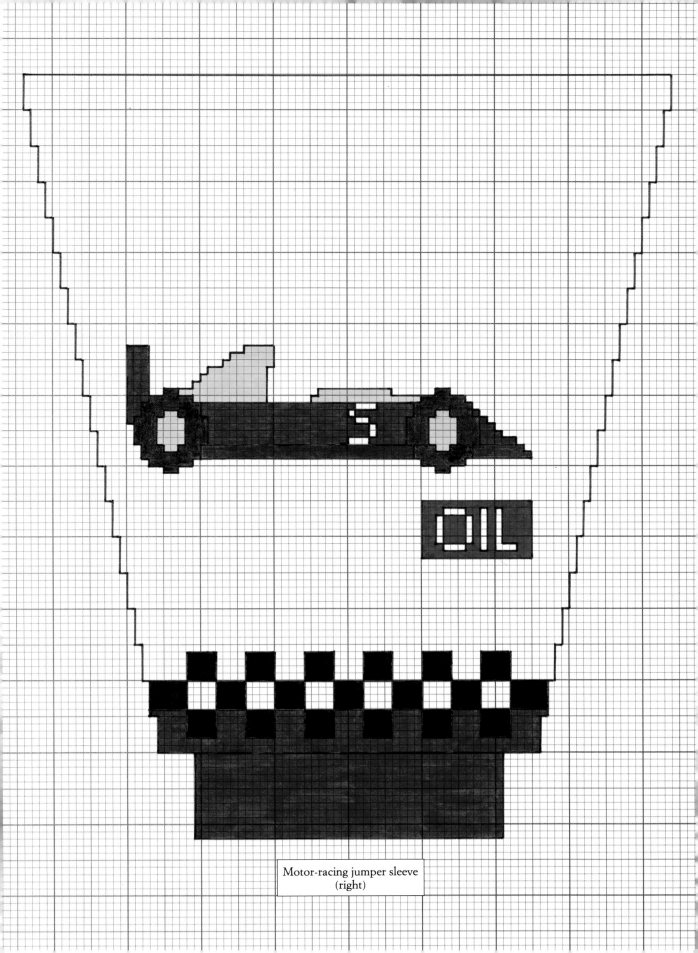

Motor-racing jumper sleeve
(right)

Motor-racing glossary

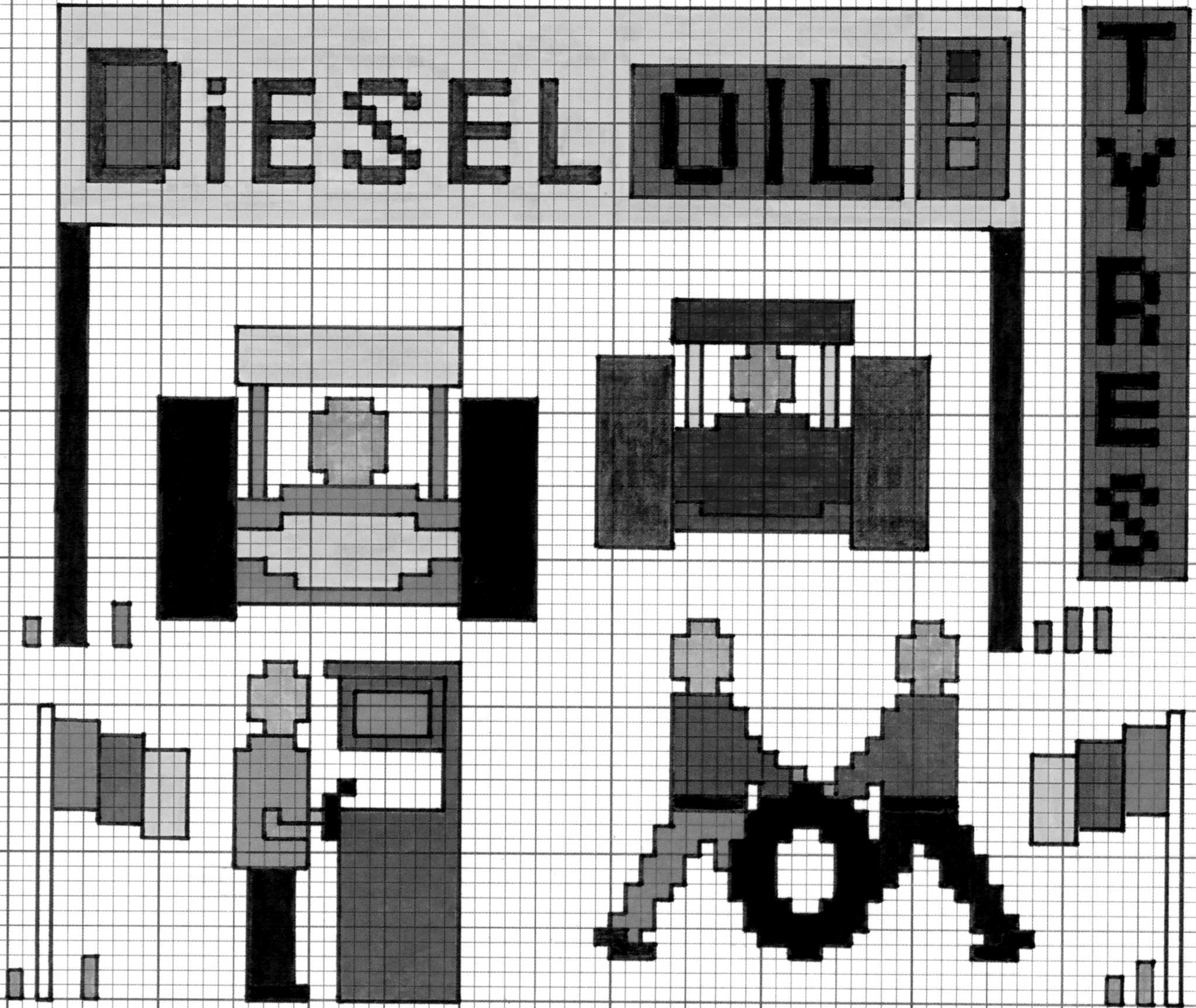

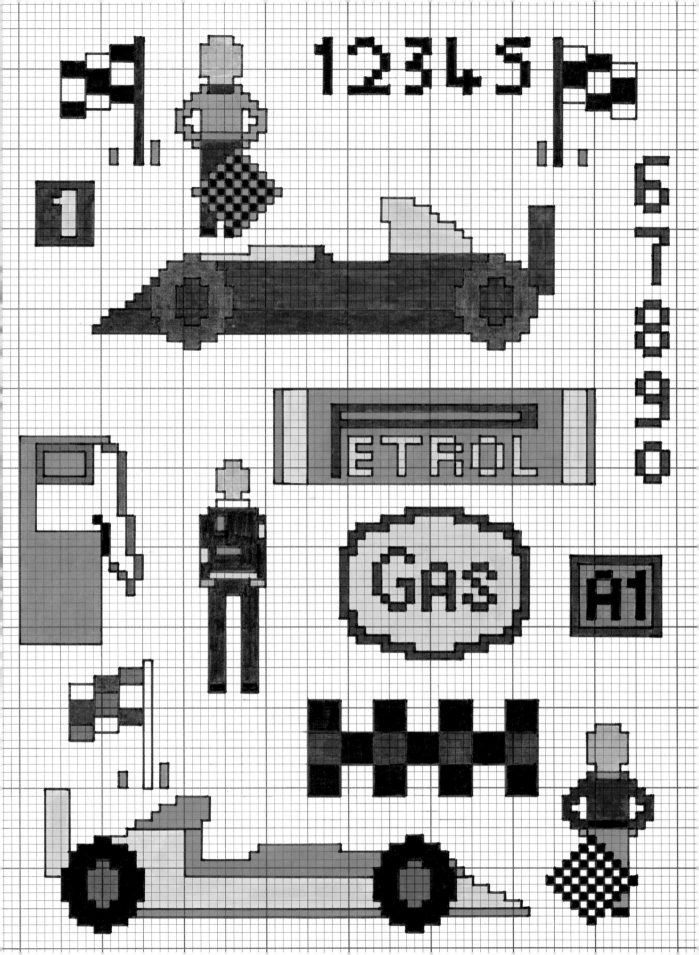

3
BASIC HANDKNITTING PATTERNS

The following patterns are of a simple and basic shape and all have dropped shoulders. As the garment is secondary to the picture it is to carry, this style was considered the most suitable for this purpose. It is easier to show a complicated picture on a simple style pattern than to attempt to match a picture to a difficult pattern. After all, the picture displayed on the garment is the main objective and on a simple background will be seen at its best.

The patterns are laid out in easy-to-follow charts and cover six sizes that range from small child to large adult, using either double-knit cotton or aran-weight wool. Both the cotton and wool are colour-banded separately for easier reading. The sizes are based upon the tension table that is shown at the start of each pattern, so do ensure that your tension is correct, adjusting needle sizes to suit if necessary. Further help on this subject can be found on page 16.

A simple way to use the patterns is to have the page photocopied, then, using a coloured pen or pencil, highlight the size required. This will ensure that you knit the correct line of figures only. Where the sleeve and body lengths need to differ from those in the pattern, simply make the necessary adjustments to suit. Increase or decrease body lengths to those required to obtain a proper fit. When shortening sleeve lengths it may be necessary to make the increase rows closer together – if the size being knitted indicates that you need to increase every fifth row, you may need to increase every fourth row in order to fit in the required number of increases to ensure finishing with the correct number of stitches.

Left Lorenzo's 'Golf' jumper is in the style of crew neck with tunic bottom (page 47). After completing the hem from the tunic bottom pattern, continue using the pattern for the crew neck.

Right 'Horse racing' in crew neck, rib bottom using chunky weight cotton (page 43). Knitted on 4mm needles for rib and 5mm needles for st st. Tension is 16 sts and 23 rows to 10cm st st. Knit to preferred size.

YARN QUANTITIES

Yarn quantities are approximate and are based on
the use of one colour only for each garment.

	WOOL			COTTON	
	Children			*Children*	
Small	61cm (24in)	400g (14oz)	Small	61cm (24in)	450g (16oz)
Medium	71cm (28in)	450g (16oz)	Medium	71cm (28in)	500g (18oz)
Large	81cm (32in)	500g (18oz)	Large	81cm (32in)	550g (20oz)
	Adults			*Adults*	
Small	102cm (40in)	800g (28oz)	Small	102cm (40in)	850g (30oz)
Medium	112cm (44in)	850g (30oz)	Medium	112cm (44in)	900g (32oz)
Large	122cm (48in)	950g (34oz)	Large	122cm (48in)	1000g (35oz)

ABBREVIATIONS

cont	continue		p	purl
dec	decrease		psso	pass slipped stitch over
inc	increase		rem	remain
k	knit		sl1	slip 1
k2 tog	knit 2 together		st	stitch
m1	make one – ie lift loop lying between		st st	stocking stitch
	needle points, place on left-hand needle,		tbl	through back of loop
	work into back		tog	together

CONVERSIONS
NEEDLE CHART

Imperial	Metric	USA		Imperial	Metric	USA
000	10	15		7	4½	7
00	9	13		8	4	6
0	8	11		9	3¾	4
1	7½	11		10	3¼	3
2	7	10½		11	3	2
3	6½	10½		12	2¾	1
4	6	10		13	2¼	0
5	5½	9		14	2	00
6	5	8				

METRIC CONVERSIONS

To convert centimetres into inches multiply by 0.3937. To convert inches into centimetres multiply by 2.54. Round figures up or down to the nearest whole or half measurement.

Examples:

20cm x 0.3937 = 7.874 or 8in
20in x 2.54 = 50.8 or 51cm

Crew Neck Rib Bottom

		Knit	Children			Adults		
Aran weight wool (Yellow) 3¾mm and 4½mm needles								
Double Knit cotton (Pink) 3¼mm and 4mm needles								
Tension	Aran weight wool 21st 26 rows to 10cm in st st 4½mm needles							
	Double knit cotton 22st 30 rows to 10cm in st st 4mm needles							
Dimension details	To fit chest size	cm	61	71	81	102	112	122
	For conversions see page 42	(in)	(24)	(28)	(32)	(40)	(44)	(48)
	Length from neckband	cm	41	47	53	71	73	75
	to bottom (back and front)		41	47	53	69	71	74
	Sleeve length	cm	28	35	40	52	54	54
			28	35	40	50	52	52
START OF PATTERN								
Body Back and front the same	Cast on with 3¾mm needles	Stitches	66	74	84	112	120	130
	Cast on with 3¼mm needles		72	82	92	114	124	134
	Work in K1 P1 rib for	Rows	12	12	12	16	16	16
			12	12	12	16	16	16
	Change to 4½mm needles	Rows	93	107	123	162	166	172
	Change to 4mm needles		108	126	144	182	188	194
	Work in st st							
Right neck and shoulder shaping	Next row knit	Stitches	24	27	31	44	48	52
			26	30	35	45	50	55
	Turn and leave remaining stitches on spare needle							
	Cast off 1 stitch at neck edge for next	Rows	6	6	7	8	8	8
			6	7	8	8	8	8
	This leaves	Stitches	18	21	24	36	40	44
			20	23	27	37	42	47
	Continue working on these stitches for	Rows	1	1	0	1	1	1
			1	0	1	1	1	1
	This ensures ending with a right side facing for shoulder shaping							
	*Cast off at beginning of next row	Stitches	6	7	8	12	14	15
			7	8	9	12	15	16
	Work one row* Repeat from * to * then cast off remaining stitches							
	With right side facing slip centre	Stitches	18	20	22	24	24	24
	stitches onto spare needle		20	22	22	24	24	24

			1	2	3	4	5	6
Left neck and shoulder shaping	Rejoin yarn to remaining stitches and work to end of row							
	Work	Rows	1	1	0	1	1	1
			1	0	1	1	1	1
	Work as right side remembering to reverse shaping							
Sleeves	Cast on with 3¾mm needles	Stitches	40	40	42	49	49	49
	Cast on with 3¼mm needles		40	42	44	49	49	49
	Work in K1 P1 rib for	Rows	12	12	12	16	16	16
			12	12	12	16	16	16
	In last row of rib increase evenly across row	Stitches	6	8	10	20	20	20
			8	8	10	20	20	20
	Change to 4½mm needles – st st							
	Change to 4mm needles – st st							
	Increase 1 stitch at each end of every following 4th or 5th row as shown	Rows	4	5	5	5	5	5
			4	4	5	5	5	5
	Continue to knit until reaching	Stitches	72	80	88	111	113	113
			78	86	96	119	121	123
	Sleeves to measure	cm	28	35	40	52	54	54
			28	35	40	50	52	52
	Cast off. Join right shoulder seam							
Neck border	Right side facing. Pick up and knit. Using 3¾mm needles. Using 3¼mm needles							
	From left front neck	Stitches	9	10	11	12	12	12
			10	10	11	12	13	13
	From centre front spare needle	Stitches	18	20	22	24	24	24
			20	22	22	24	24	24
	Up right front neck to shoulder seam	Stitches	9	10	11	12	12	12
			10	10	11	12	13	13
	From right back neck	Stitches	8	9	10	12	12	12
			9	9	10	12	12	12
	From centre back spare needle	Stitches	18	20	22	24	24	24
			20	22	22	24	24	24
	From left back neck	Stitches	8	9	10	12	12	12
			9	9	10	12	12	12
	Work in K1 P1 rib for	cm	6	6	6	7	7	7
			6	6	6	7	7	7
	Loosely cast off in rib							
	Using 4½mm needles							
	Using 4mm needles							

HAND KNIT

'V' Neck Cardigan

Aran weight wool (Yellow) 3¾mm and 4½mm needles								
Double knit cotton (Pink) 3¼mm and 4mm needles								
Tension	Aran 21st 26 rows to 10 cm in st st 4½mm needles							
	Cotton 22st 30 rows to 10 cm in st st 4mm needles							
		Knit	Children			Adults		
Dimension details	To fit chest size	cm	61	71	81	102	112	122
	For conversions see page 42	(in)	(24)	(28)	(32)	(40)	(44)	(48)
	Length from neckband	cm	41	47	53	71	73	75
	to bottom (back and front)		41	47	53	69	71	74
	Sleeve length	cm	28	35	40	52	54	54
			28	35	40	50	52	52
START OF PATTERN								
Back body and shoulder shaping	Cast on with 3¾mm needles	Stitches	66	74	84	112	120	130
	Cast on with 3¼mm needles		72	82	92	114	124	134
	Work in K1 P1 rib for	Rows	12	12	12	16	16	16
			12	12	12	16	16	16
	Change to 4½mm needles	Rows	100	112	130	170	174	180
	Change to 4mm needles		112	134	152	190	196	202
	Work in st st for							
	Cast off at beginning of next 4 rows	Stitches	6	7	8	12	14	15
			7	8	9	12	15	16
	Cast off at beginning of next 2 rows	Stitches	6	7	8	12	12	14
			6	7	9	13	12	15
	Cast off remaining stitches							
Right front body	Cast on with 3¾mm needles	Stitches	37	41	45	65	69	74
	Cast on with 3¼mm needles		40	45	50	65	71	76
	Work K1 P1 for	Rows	12	12	12	16	16	16
			12	12	12	16	16	16
	Change to 4½mm needles	Rows	66	76	78	89	91	95
	Change to 4mm needles		76	78	84	103	105	109
	Work in st st							
	But continue in rib along	Stitches	7	7	7	9	9	9
	front edges for		7	7	7	9	9	9

These rib stitches form the band to hold the buttons and button holes.
Work this number button holes evenly spaces on appropriate side of rib band, starting
on third row of lower rib, finishing last button hole 2 rows before neck shaping starts

	Number of button holes		6	6	6	9	9	9
	Work to end of	Row	66	76	78	89	91	95
			76	78	84	103	105	109
Right front neck and shoulder shaping	Continuing rib band as before, Dec 1 st at neck edge on first st after rib band or last st before rib band on next and every following	Rows						
			2	2	3	3	3	3
			2	3	3	3	3	3
	Until left with	Stitches	18	21	24	36	40	44
	(plus rib band)		20	23	27	37	42	47
	When you have worked the same number of rows as back cast off for shoulder shaping							
	Cast off at armhole edge	Stitches	6	7	8	13	14	15
	of next 2 alternative rows		7	8	9	12	15	16
	Work one row. Cast off remaining stitches (leaving rib band stitches on a safety pin)							
Left front body	Knit as for front right, reversing all shapings							
Sleeves	Cast on with 3¾mm needles	Stitches	40	40	42	49	49	49
	Cast on with 3¼mm needles		40	42	44	49	49	49
	Work in K1 P1 rib for	Rows	12	12	12	16	16	16
			12	12	12	16	16	16
	In last row of rib	Stitches	6	8	10	20	20	20
	inc evenly across row		6	8	10	20	20	20
	Change to 4¾mm needles – st st – Change to 4mm needles – st st							
	Inc 1 st at each end of every following	Rows	4	5	5	5	5	5
	4th or 5th row as shown		4	4	5	5	5	5
	Continue to knit until reaching	Stitches	72	80	88	11	113	113
			78	86	96	119	121	123
	Sleeves to measure	cm	28	35	40	52	54	54
			28	35	40	50	52	52
Shoulder neck border	Cast off. Join shoulder seams							
	Using 4½mm or 4mm needles, pick up stitches from safety pin and knit one side of of front rib band until when slightly stretched it reaches centre back. Cast off. Knit other side to match. Stitch rib band in position							

<u>HAND KNIT</u>

Roll Neck Tunic Bottom

			Children			Adults		
Aran weight wool (Yellow) 3¾mm and 4½mm needles								
Double knit cotton (Pink) 3¼mm and 4mm needles								
Tension	Aran 21sts, 26 rows to 10 cm in st st, using 4½mm needles								
	Cotton 22sts, 30 rows to 10 cm in st st, using 4mm needles								
			Children			Adults		
Dimension details	To fit chest size	cm	61	71	81	102	112	122
	For conversions see page 42	(in)	(24)	(28)	(32)	(40)	(44)	(48)
	Length from neckband	cm	41	47	53	71	73	75
	to bottom (back and front)		41	47	53	69	71	74
	sleeve length	cm	28	35	40	52	54	54
			28	35	40	50	52	52
START OF PATTERN								
Front hem (back and front the same)	Cast on with 3¾mm needles	Stitches	66	74	84	112	120	130
	Cast on with 3¼mm needles		72	82	92	114	124	134
	Work in st st for	Rows	11	11	13	15	15	17
	finishing with a knit row		11	13	13	17	17	17
Work one further knit row								
	Work in st st	Rows	10	10	12	14	14	16
	commencing with a knit row		10	12	12	16	16	16
Next row knit. This row forms hem. Pick up 1 stitch from casting on row and 1 stitch from needle and knit together to end of row								
Front body	Change to 4½mm needles	Rows	88	102	118	162	166	172
	Change to 4mm needles		102	120	138	182	188	194
	and work in st st for								
Front right neck and shoulder shaping	Next row knit	Stitches	24	27	31	44	48	52
			26	30	35	45	50	55
Turn and leave remaining stitches on spare needle								
	Cast off 1 stitch at neck	Rows	6	6	7	8	8	8
	edge for next		6	7	8	8	8	8
	This leaves	Stitches	18	21	24	36	40	44
			20	23	27	37	42	47
	Continue working on these	Row	1	1	0	1	1	1
	stitches for		1	0	1	1	1	1
This ensures ending with a right side facing for shoulder shaping								

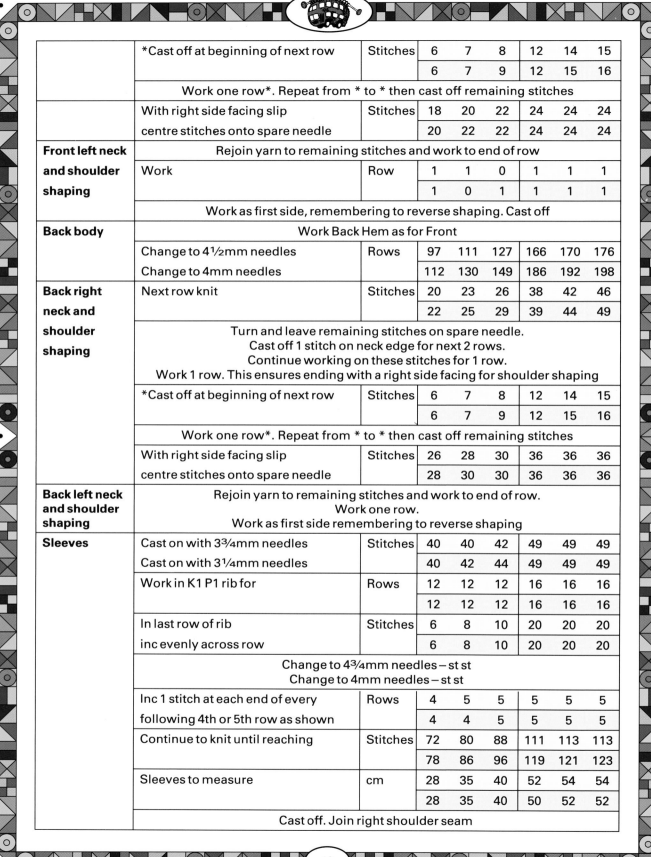

			Size 1	Size 2	Size 3	Size 4	Size 5	Size 6
	*Cast off at beginning of next row	Stitches	6	7	8	12	14	15
			6	7	9	12	15	16
	Work one row*. Repeat from * to * then cast off remaining stitches							
	With right side facing slip	Stitches	18	20	22	24	24	24
	centre stitches onto spare needle		20	22	22	24	24	24
Front left neck and shoulder shaping	Rejoin yarn to remaining stitches and work to end of row							
	Work	Row	1	1	0	1	1	1
			1	0	1	1	1	1
	Work as first side, remembering to reverse shaping. Cast off							
Back body	Work Back Hem as for Front							
	Change to 4½mm needles	Rows	97	111	127	166	170	176
	Change to 4mm needles		112	130	149	186	192	198
Back right neck and shoulder shaping	Next row knit	Stitches	20	23	26	38	42	46
			22	25	29	39	44	49
	Turn and leave remaining stitches on spare needle. Cast off 1 stitch on neck edge for next 2 rows. Continue working on these stitches for 1 row. Work 1 row. This ensures ending with a right side facing for shoulder shaping							
	*Cast off at beginning of next row	Stitches	6	7	8	12	14	15
			6	7	9	12	15	16
	Work one row*. Repeat from * to * then cast off remaining stitches							
	With right side facing slip	Stitches	26	28	30	36	36	36
	centre stitches onto spare needle		28	30	30	36	36	36
Back left neck and shoulder shaping	Rejoin yarn to remaining stitches and work to end of row. Work one row. Work as first side remembering to reverse shaping							
Sleeves	Cast on with 3¾mm needles	Stitches	40	40	42	49	49	49
	Cast on with 3¼mm needles		40	42	44	49	49	49
	Work in K1 P1 rib for	Rows	12	12	12	16	16	16
			12	12	12	16	16	16
	In last row of rib	Stitches	6	8	10	20	20	20
	inc evenly across row		6	8	10	20	20	20
	Change to 4¾mm needles – st st / Change to 4mm needles – st st							
	Inc 1 stitch at each end of every	Rows	4	5	5	5	5	5
	following 4th or 5th row as shown		4	4	5	5	5	5
	Continue to knit until reaching	Stitches	72	80	88	111	113	113
			78	86	96	119	121	123
	Sleeves to measure	cm	28	35	40	52	54	54
			28	35	40	50	52	52
	Cast off. Join right shoulder seam							

Neck border	With right side facing. Pick up and knit:								
Using 3¾mm needles From left	Stitches	9	10	11	12	12	12
Using 3¼mm needles front neck		10	10	11	12	13	13
From centre front	Stitches	18	20	22	24	24	24
spare needle		20	22	22	24	24	24
Up right front neck	Stitches	9	10	11	12	12	12
to shoulder seam		10	10	11	12	13	13
From right back neck	Stitches	4	5	6	6	6	6
		4	6	6	6	6	6
From centre back	Stitches	26	28	30	36	36	36
spare needle		28	30	30	36	36	36
From left back neck	Stitches	4	5	6	6	6	6
		4	6	6	6	6	6
Work in K1 P1 rib for	Rows	6	6	6	8	8	8
		6	6	6	8	8	8
Beg with a p row	Rows	6	6	6	8	8	8
work in st st for		6	6	6	8	8	8
Using 4½mm needles	Loosely cast off in st st						
Using 4mm needles							

MAKING UP

Making up your garment is very simple, taking a minimum of skill but a large amount of care. The final appearance of the finished jumper can be marred by sloppy or indifferent workmanship that would waste the long hours you spent knitting with loving care and attention. It is crucial that the seams are joined evenly using the correct amount of tension. Stitching the seams too tightly gives a gathered look and stitching too loosely is likely to cause holes to appear at a very early stage of wear. Do not fall into the trap of having completed your last sleeve, at the same time that dinner is due, then rushing the making up in order to see your creation completed. Take this operation slowly and carefully.

The first step to making up your garment is to sew in all loose ends on back, front and sleeves (page 20). It is most important that all ends are very well secured before you proceed further.

Lightly press with an iron according to ball band instructions prior to sewing up.

For sewing up seams, use either your own method that you are familiar with or one of the methods shown on page 21.

FOR CREW NECK WITH BOTTOM AND CUFF RIB

Sew up left shoulder seam, including neckband, to match right shoulder seam, already sewn up as in pattern. Place centre of cast-off edge of sleeve to shoulder seam. Stitch along full length of cast-off edge of sleeve, attaching sleeve to shoulder. Repeat this procedure for the second sleeve. Starting again at left bottom rib, sew together back and front until underarm is reached. Continue down sleeve to cuff. Repeat this for the right side. Fold neckband in half and stitch loosely in place on the wrong side.

FOR V-NECK CARDIGAN

Place centre of cast-off edge of sleeve to shoulder seam. Stitch along full length of cast-off edge of sleeve, attaching sleeve to shoulder. Repeat this procedure for the second sleeve. Starting at left bottom rib, sew together back and front until underarm is reached. Continue down sleeve to cuff. Repeat this for the right side. Sew buttons securely in place.

FOR ROLL NECK WITH TUNIC BOTTOM

Sew up left shoulder seam, including neck, to match right shoulder seam, already sewn up as in pattern. Place centre of cast-off edge of sleeve to shoulder seam. Stitch along full length of cast-off edge of sleeve, attaching sleeve to shoulder. Repeat this procedure for the second sleeve. Starting again at left bottom hem, sew together back and front until underarm is reached. Continue down sleeve to cuff. Repeat this for the right side. It is intended that the neck is *not* stitched down, allowing it to roll naturally with wrong side of st st showing.

FINGER PUPPETS AND DOLLS

If finger puppets or dolls have been made, it is advisable to attach them to the jumper with short lengths of wool so that they do not become lost.

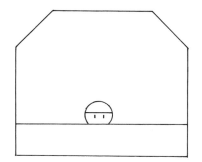

Left 'Borders with people' shows what a wonderful effect may be obtained by the use of simple border patterns. Here we have combined the crew neck with the tunic bottom. After completing the hem continue with the crew neck pattern.

4
HATS, SOCKS AND MITTENS

When people ask me to design a garment for them incorporating interpretations of their own ideas, they often also request matching accessories such as hats, socks and mittens. One example of this demand is the haunted Scottish castle that sells matching jumpers and hats for children and adults sporting both stuffed-head ghosts and pull-out ghost dolls.

Because I am so frequently asked for matching accessories, I have included instructions on how to make hats, socks and mittens that will fit your own style or designs.

The hat shown in this chapter can be knitted using a variety of colours and graph designs. We have shown it on page 85 where it matches the Christmas jumper and has a pull-out Father Christmas in the pocket. Again our mittens and

Hats

Aran weight wool 3¾mm and 4½mm needles
Tension 21 sts, 26 rows to 10cm in st st, using 4½mm needles
Size 42cm (16½in) around head, 26cm (10in) long

Main part	Cast on using 3¾mm needles	Stitches	96
	Work in st st	Rows	12
	Change to 4½mm needles Cont in st st for	Rows	52
	A pocket can be inserted if required after 20 rows worked		
Top shaping	K7, *sl 1, k2 tog, psso, k7, repeat from * to last 6 sts, k6		
	Work in st st	Rows	3
	K6, *sl 1, k2 tog, psso, k5, repeat from * to last 5 sts, k5		
	Work in st st	Rows	3
	K5, *sl 1, k2 tog, psso, k3, repeat from * to last 4 sts, k4		
	Work in st st	Rows	3
	K1, *sl 1, k2 tog, psso, k1, repeat from * to last st, k1		
	Work in st st	Rows	3
	K2 tog, repeat to end of row		
	Thread yarn through remaining 11 sts and fasten off		
Making up	Sew side seam. Make 3 plaited lengths of wool with tassels and fasten securely in place		

socks are shown using various graphs. The socks showing the Easter egg with chicken and the chimney with Father Christmas could be knitted singly and then packed with small festive presents for the appropriate occasion.

The patterns for the socks and mittens are in three children's sizes, while the hat will fit children of most ages. The pattern for knitting socks uses two needles only and, as socks are knitted from top to toe, do remember when joining in graphs to commence at the top of the graph and not at the bottom.

HANDY HINT
When working out a design for socks and mittens remember to knit the pattern to come on the outside – on the back of each mitten and on different sides of opposite socks.

Hannah is pegging up a selection of ideas for socks and mittens using our basic patterns. She is wearing a jumper featuring alphabet letters taken from the Picture Library.

Socks

Double knit wool	2 pairs of double-pointed 3¼mm needles				
Tension	26 sts, 34 rows to 10cm in st st				

Foot sizes For conversions see page 42		cm (in)	15 (6)	17 (7)	20 (8)
Ankle	Cast on	Sts	44	44	50
	Work in k1, p1, rib for	Rows	2	2	3
	Work in st st for	Rows	13	13	15
	Work in k1, p1, rib for	Rows	12	12	17
	Work in st st for	Rows	10	20	28
Dec row	K1, sl1, k1, psso, k to last 3 sts, k2 tog, k1				
	*Work in st st for	Rows	9	9	14
	Repeat dec row*				
	Repeat from * to * once				
	Sts remaining	Sts	38	38	44
	Work in st st for	Rows	11	11	11
Foot	Divide for heel, k	Sts	9	9	10
	Sl on to spare yarn, leave for instep	Sts	20	20	24
	Sl on to end of needle	Sts	9	9	10
	(outside edges meeting in centre)				
	Work in st st for	Rows	15	15	15
	K	Sts	13	13	15
	Turn, p	Sts	8	8	10
	Turn, k	Sts	7	7	9
	K2 tog, turn				
	P	Sts	7	7	9
	P2 tog, turn				
	Cont dec in this way until remains	Sts	8	8	10
	K 1 row				
	Next row pick up and knit 11 sts down side of heel				
	P	Sts	19	19	21
	Pick up and p 11 sts down heel, turn. You now have	Sts	30	30	32
	Work 2 rows st st				
	K1, k2 tog, k to last 3 sts, sl1, k1, psso, k1				
	Next row p				
	Repeat last 2 rows until	Sts	18	18	20
	Cont in st st until foot measures from heel pick-up point	cm	7.5	10	12.75

Shape toe	Sl1, k1, psso, k to last 2 sts, k2 tog				
	Next row p				
	Rep last 2 rows until	Sts	8	8	10
	K2 tog across row, leave sts on yarn				
	Rejoin yarn to instep sts				
	Starting with p row, work st st	Rows	14	14	14
	Cont in st st until instep measures same as sole, ending with a k row				
	(1st and 2nd size) p5, p2 tog, p6, p2 tog, p5	Sts	18	18	–
	(3rd size) (p3, p2 tog) twice, p4, (p2 tog, p3) twice	Sts	–	–	20
	K2 tog, k to last 2 sts, sl1, k1, psso				
	Next row p				
	Rep last 2 rows until	Sts	8	8	10
	K2 tog across sts				
	Slip sts from yarn on to another needle				
	Using a 3rd size 3¼mm needle, take first st from each needle, p2 tog across, casting off as you go				

Making up
Join side seams and back seam

Mittens

Double knit wool 3¼mm and 4mm needles
Tension 24 sts, 32 rows to 10cm in st st, using 4mm needles

			S	M	L
Approx length For conversions see page 42	cm (in)		15 (6)	18 (7)	21 (8)
Right mitten	Using 3¼mm needles cast on	Sts	37	39	41
	Work in k1, p1 rib for Change to 4mm needles and st st *	Rows	12	14	16
Gusset Inc row	K	Sts	20	21	22
	P1, m1, k1, m1, p1				
	K	Sts	14	15	16
Row 2	P	Sts	14	15	16
	K1, p3, k1				
	P	Sts	20	21	22

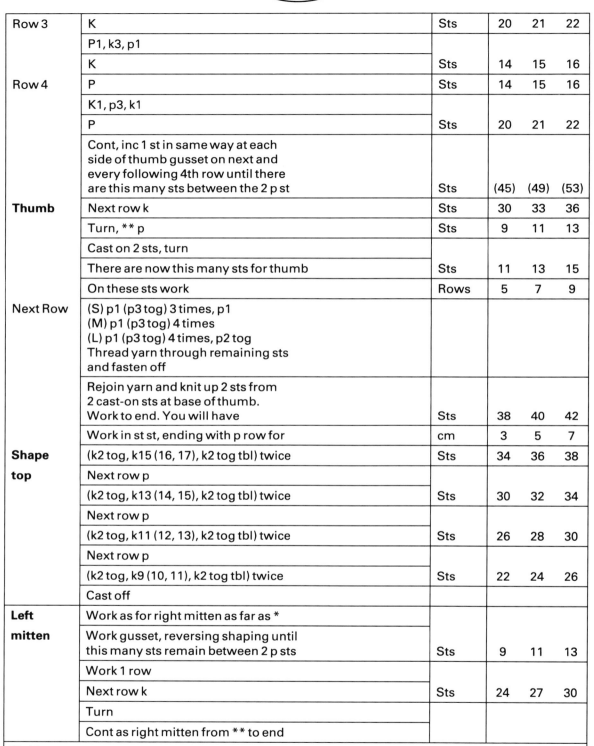

			Sts	20	21	22
Row 3	K					
	P1, k3, p1					
	K		Sts	14	15	16
Row 4	P		Sts	14	15	16
	K1, p3, k1					
	P		Sts	20	21	22
	Cont, inc 1 st in same way at each side of thumb gusset on next and every following 4th row until there are this many sts between the 2 p st		Sts	(45)	(49)	(53)
Thumb	Next row k		Sts	30	33	36
	Turn, ** p		Sts	9	11	13
	Cast on 2 sts, turn					
	There are now this many sts for thumb		Sts	11	13	15
	On these sts work		Rows	5	7	9
Next Row	(S) p1 (p3 tog) 3 times, p1 (M) p1 (p3 tog) 4 times (L) p1 (p3 tog) 4 times, p2 tog Thread yarn through remaining sts and fasten off					
	Rejoin yarn and knit up 2 sts from 2 cast-on sts at base of thumb. Work to end. You will have		Sts	38	40	42
	Work in st st, ending with p row for		cm	3	5	7
Shape	(k2 tog, k15 (16, 17), k2 tog tbl) twice		Sts	34	36	38
top	Next row p					
	(k2 tog, k13 (14, 15), k2 tog tbl) twice		Sts	30	32	34
	Next row p					
	(k2 tog, k11 (12, 13), k2 tog tbl) twice		Sts	26	28	30
	Next row p					
	(k2 tog, k9 (10, 11), k2 tog tbl) twice		Sts	22	24	26
	Cast off					
Left	Work as for right mitten as far as *					
mitten	Work gusset, reversing shaping until this many sts remain between 2 p sts		Sts	9	11	13
	Work 1 row					
	Next row k		Sts	24	27	30
	Turn					
	Cont as right mitten from ** to end					

Making up
Join seams matching shape

5

BASIC MACHINE KNITTING PATTERNS

As I felt that the knitting of picture jumpers should not remain the prerogative of just the handknitter, machine knitting versions of identical patterns have been included. These are purely for machine knitters who consider themselves sufficiently experienced to tackle this type of garment. To illustrate how this same design is made using both hand- and machine knitting, the small child's jumper is shown on page 85 in two colourways.

All the machine knitting patterns included here are basic and all have dropped shoulders for greater simplicity. They allow for the use of both cotton and wool yarns with the pattern colour highlighted for easier reading.

The pattern covers six sizes ranging from small child to large adult, based upon the tension displayed, so be sure to knit a tension square first.

As always happens with machine knitting, graphs come out mirror-imaged and although this does not affect the finished garment's picture design, it does affect words or letters, so bear this in mind from the outset when designing your graph. Also, when knitting sleeves, commence at the top of the graph and not at the bottom.

INSTRUCTIONS FOR POCKET

Cast off 7 sts where pocket top is to appear. Put these needles into working position, put all other needles into holding position. Pick up 7 sts, 13 rows below, and put on needles in working position. Knit 13 rows on these sts. Break yarn. Take carriage to end. Hold position off. Recommence knitting.

YARN QUANTITIES

Yarn quantities are approximate and are based on the use of one colour only for each garment.

WOOL
Children
Small	61cm (24in)	400g (14oz)
Medium	71cm (28in)	450g (16oz)
Large	81cm (32in)	500g (18oz)

Adults
Small	102cm (40cm)	600g (21oz)
Medium	112cm (44in)	650g (23oz)
Large	122cm (48in)	700g (25oz)

COTTON
Children
Small	61cm (24in)	450g (16oz)
Medium	71cm (28in)	500g (18oz)
Large	81cm (32in)	550g (20oz)

Adults
Small	102cm (40in)	800g (28oz)
Medium	112cm (44in)	850g (30oz)
Large	122cm (48in)	900g (32oz)

HANDY HINT

It is very important to work a separate tension square with the intarsia carriage.

ABBREVIATIONS

cont	continue	RT	rib tension
MT	main tension	st	stitch
RC	row counter	TD	tension dial

This very striking flower cardigan worn by Sian was
created using the basic cardigan pattern with flowers
from the Picture Library.

MACHINE KNIT

'V' Neck Cardigan

Aran weight wool (Yellow)		Double knit cotton (Pink)					
Tension	Aran 19 sts, 27 rows to 10 cm in st st						
	Cotton 19½ sts, 24 rows to 10 cm in st st						
			Children			Adults	
Dimension	To fit chest size	cm	61	71	81	102	112	122
details	For conversions see page 42	(in)	(24)	(28)	(32)	(40)	(44)	(48)
	Length from neckband	cm	41	47	53	71	73	75
	to bottom (back and front)		41	47	53	71	73	75
	Sleeve length	cm	28	35	40	52	54	54
			28	35	40	52	54	54
START OF PATTERN								
Back body	1x1 rib cast on	Stitches	58	66	76	94	104	110
			60	70	80	100	110	114
	Work RT for	Rows	12	12	12	16	16	16
			12	12	12	16	16	16
	Transfer to main bed		46	56	66	96	100	102
	MT RC.000 work to RC		36	48	60	82	84	88
	Place marker at each end of row							
	Work to RC		96	112	130	174	182	188
			84	98	112	156	160	166
Shoulder	On next 6 rows, hold	Stitches	7	8	9	10	11	12
shaping			7	8	9	11	12	13
	Take shoulder stitches off onto waste yarn							
	Take neck sts	Stitches	16	18	22	34	38	38
	off onto waste yarn		18	22	26	34	38	36
Front body	1x1 rib cast on	Stitches	30	34	40	46	52	54
(left)			30	36	40	50	56	58
	Work as back to RC		46	56	66	96	100	102
			36	48	60	82	84	88
	Place marker at each end of row							
	Dec 1 stitch at neck edge on next	Row	5	5	5	4	4	4
	and every following		4	4	4	4	4	4
	Until remain	Stitches	21	24	27	30	33	36
			21	24	27	33	36	39

	Continue to RC		96	112	130	174	182	188
			84	98	112	156	160	166
Shoulder shaping	As back. Take off onto waste yarn.							
Front body (right)	Knit right front, reversing all shapings. Place back and fronts on machine, right sides together, knit 1 row TD 10 across all stitches. Latchet off							
Sleeves	Pick up between markers	Stitches	64	72	80	106	108	110
			64	72	80	106	108	110
	Decreasing 1 stitch at end every 5th row to	Stitches	40	42	44	58	60	62
			42	44	48	62	62	64
	Continue to RC		62	82	96	120	124	124
			56	72	84	110	116	116
	Take off onto waste yarn and		30	34	36	42	44	46
	rehang onto main bed over stitches		30	34	36	42	44	46
	Knit 1 row							
	Transfer to ribber	Rows	12	12	12	16	16	16
	1x1 RT knit		12	12	12	16	16	16
	Knit 1 row TD $^{10}/_{10}$ Transfer to main bed. Latchet off							
Button band	Using full needle rib cast on	Stitches	11	11	11	15	15	15
			11	11	11	15	15	15
	Knit band on rib tension making 2 stitches buttonholes up to the marker on the front edge and continuing to correct length							

MACHINE KNIT

Crew Neck Rib Bottom

	Aran weight wool (Yellow)			**Double knit cotton** (Pink)				
Tension	Aran 19 sts, 27 rows to 10 cm							
	Cotton 19½ sts, 24 rows to 10 cm							
				Children			Adults	
Dimension details	To fit chest size	cm	61	71	81	102	112	122
	For conversions see page 42	(in)	(24)	(28)	(32)	(40)	(44)	(48)
	Length from neckband	cm	41	47	53	71	73	75
	to bottom (back and front)		41	47	53	71	73	75
	Sleeve length	cm	28	35	40	52	54	54
			28	35	40	52	54	54

START OF PATTERN								
Body (Back and front the same)	1x1 rib cast on	Stitches	58	66	76	94	104	110
			60	70	80	100	110	114
	Work RT for	Rows	12	12	12	16	16	16
			12	12	12	16	16	16
	Transfer to main bed		46	56	66	96	100	102
	MT RC.000 work to RC		36	48	60	82	84	88
	Place marker at each end of row							
	Work to RC		92	108	126	168	176	182
			80	94	108	150	154	160
Neck shaping	Hold centre and all stitches to left	Stitches	8	10	14	22	26	26
			10	14	18	22	26	24
	Working on right side only carriage on right – hold one stitch on neck edge on next	Rows	4	4	4	6	6	6
			4	4	4	6	6	6
	Stitches remaining		21	24	27	30	33	36
			21	24	27	33	36	39
	Knit 1 row – carriage at left							
Shoulder shaping	On next 2 alternate rows, hold	Stitches	7	8	9	10	11	12
			7	8	9	11	12	13
	Knit 1 row across all stitches and take off onto waste yarn. Knit other side reversing all shapings. Take neck stitches off onto waste yarn. Join one shoulder							
Neckband	1x1 rib cast on	Stitches	56	64	72	88	100	104
			56	64	72	88	100	104
	Work RT for	Rows	6	6	6	8	8	8
			6	6	6	8	8	8
	Transfer to main bed. Pick up stitches from back and front and place over neckband. Knit 1 row TD 10. Latchet off. Join other shoulder							
Sleeves	Pick up between markers	Stitches	64	72	80	106	108	110
			64	72	80	106	108	110
	Decreasing 1 stitch at each end every 5th row to	Stitches	40	42	44	58	60	62
			42	44	48	62	62	64
	Continue to RC		62	82	96	120	124	124
			56	72	84	110	116	116
	Take off onto waste yarn and rehang onto main bed over stitches		30	34	36	42	44	46
			30	34	36	42	44	46
	Knit 1 row							
	Transfer to ribber 1x1 RT knit	Rows	12	12	12	16	16	16
			12	12	12	16	16	16
	Knit 1 row TD $^{10}/_{10}$. Transfer to main bed. Latchet off							

Roll Neck Tunic Bottom

	Aran weight wool (Yellow)		Double knit cotton (Pink)		

				Children			Adults		
Tension	Aran 19 sts, 27 rows to 10 cm								
	Cotton 19½ sts, 24 rows to 10 cm								
Dimension details	To fit chest size	cm		61	71	81	102	112	122
	For conversions see page 42	(in)		(24)	(28)	(32)	(40)	(44)	(48)
	Length from neckband	cm		41	47	53	71	73	75
	to bottom (back and front)			41	47	53	71	73	75
	Sleeve length	cm		28	35	40	52	54	54
				28	35	40	52	54	54
START OF PATTERN									
Back body	Cast on in waste yarn	Stitches		58	66	76	94	104	110
				60	70	80	100	110	114
	Knit a few rows								
	Change to main yarn								
	MT – 1 knit	Rows		12	12	14	16	16	18
				12	12	14	16	16	18
	With the latchet tool, reverse the last row knitted to form a ridge								
	Change to main yarn								
	Knit	Rows		11	11	13	15	15	17
				11	11	13	15	15	17
	Pick up first row to form a hem			46	56	66	96	100	102
	MT RC.000 work to RC			36	48	60	82	84	88
	Place marker at each end of row								
	Work to RC			94	110	128	170	178	184
				82	96	110	152	156	162
Neck shaping	Hold centre	Stitches		12	14	18	26	30	30
	and all stitches to left			14	18	22	26	30	28
	Working on right side only carriage on right – hold one stitch on neck edge on next	Rows		2	2	2	4	4	4
				2	2	2	4	4	4
	Stitches remaining			21	24	27	30	33	36
				21	24	27	33	36	39
	Knit 1 row – carriage at left								

Shoulder shaping	On next 2 alternate rows, hold	Stitches	7	8	9	10	11	12
			7	8	9	11	12	13
	Knit 1 row across all stitches and take off onto waste yarn. Knit other side reversing all shapings. Take neck stitches off onto waste yarn							
Front body	Work as back to RC		90	106	124	166	174	180
			78	92	106	148	152	158
Neck shaping	Hold centre	Stitches	4	6	10	18	22	22
	and all stitches to left		6	10	14	18	22	20
	Working on right side only carriage on right – hold one stitch on neck edge on next	Rows	6	6	6	8	8	8
			6	6	6	8	8	8
	Stitches remaining		21	24	27	30	33	36
			21	24	27	33	36	39
	Knit 1 row – carriage at left							
Shoulder shaping	As back. Join one shoulder							
Neckband	Cast on "e" wrap	Stitches	56	60	68	92	96	100
			56	60	68	92	96	100
	MT knit	Rows	6	6	6	10	10	10
			6	6	6	10	10	10
	Transfer to ribber 1x1							
	Work RT for	Rows	6	6	6	8	8	8
			6	6	6	8	8	8
	Transfer back to main bed. Take off onto waste yarn. Turn and put back onto main bed. Place stitches of body on neckband, right sides facing. Knit 1 row TD 10. Latchet off. Join other shoulder							
Sleeves	Pick up between markers	Stitches	64	72	80	106	108	110
			64	72	80	106	108	110
	Decreasing 1 stitch at each end every 5th row to	Stitches	40	42	44	52	58	62
			42	44	48	62	62	64
	Continue to RC		62	82	96	120	124	124
			56	72	84	110	116	116
	Take off onto waste yarn and rehang onto main bed over stitches		30	34	36	42	44	46
			30	34	36	42	44	46
	Knit 1 row							
	Transfer to ribber 1x1 RT knit	Rows	12	12	12	16	16	16
			12	12	12	16	16	16
	Knit 1 row TD $^{10}/_{10}$ Transfer to main bed. Latchet off							

6

THE
FINISHING TOUCH

When designing a picture knitted garment, it is almost impossible not to have people or animals as one of its main subjects, especially when the garment has been designed purely as a fun jumper for children. Although it would be very easy to leave the animals and people in a flat, one-dimensional view, the transformation that is achieved when the figures take on a three-dimensional look is truly amazing. They really do bring life to any scene, be it jungle or street. Finger puppets, too, are very popular with younger children. These can be either people or animals and they fulfil two functions: first, they enhance the jumper's design and secondly they give children another toy to play with. I do recommend, though, that if finger puppets are used, you should attach them to the bottom of the pocket, using one or two strands of wool, which will prevent them from falling out and becoming lost.

I find that in order to portray depth, generally I require heads of three sizes, small for distance, large for foreground and medium for anywhere in between. Some need to be seen facing forwards, some to be seen from behind; some heads have short hair, some have long hair, while others have no hair at all; pony-tails, plaits and beards can all be incorporated. Of course, all of these have first to be knitted and then, after they have been stuffed with some suitable material, they can be attached to the jumper. Then, taking a darning needle with the required colour wool, stitch in such items as eyes, mouths, beards, moustaches, even pirates' eye-patches; let your imagination run free. If you decide to make a stuffed head,

when knitting the garment, knit a blank of fleshy colour pink for the place where the head is intended to be, such as those shown on the people in the Picture Library. Then, when the garment is finished, knit the heads separately to cover the blank area.

The finger puppets shown for making are a person, a duck and a crocodile, but these give only a general idea and do not cover all the possibilities. For instance, you may wish to make ghosts, Father Christmas, all types of animals and people – the choice, dictated purely by the jumper's design, is endless. In some instances it is better that finger puppets are replaced by knitted dolls which can then become an additional toy for the child to play with. Some children enjoy having puppets detached from the garment for just that reason. Fabric animals, too, make an interesting variation and contribution to the design. They are extremely simple to make using the zigzag attachment on any sewing-machine and can be run up in only a few minutes.

Stuffed heads, finger puppets, knitted dolls and fabric animals are very basic and simple to make. All the instructions are for front-facing heads using 3 1/4mm needles, and either cotton or wool. For rear-view heads, commence hair colour one row earlier than stated. As these items are so small, the need for careful tension can be relaxed.

■ ■

Our 'Noah's Ark' shows a collection of finger puppets, pull-out dolls, crocodile, material animals and stuffed heads. Hannah is wearing this my first and most successful design, which remains very much one of my favourites.

HEADS

Using 3¼mm needles and either cotton or wool in desired shade of skin colour, work in st st.

	Small	Medium	Large
Cast on	4 sts	5 sts	6 sts
1st row (all sizes) Increase 1 st at each end of row			
Work	2 rows	2 rows	3 rows
Join in hair colour yarn			
Work	2 rows	2 rows	2 rows
Next row (all sizes) Decrease 1 st at each end of row			
Next row (all sizes) Decrease 1 st at each end of row			
Next row	Fasten off leaving approx 20in (8in) for sewing in		k2 tog twice
Next row			Fasten off

OLD MAN'S HEAD

Knit head as described in previous instruction, selecting required size and using skin-coloured yarn only. When complete, sew head on to jumper (refer to the instructions for making up), then take darning needle with grey or white yarn and make small loop stitches around lower head only (Fig 1).

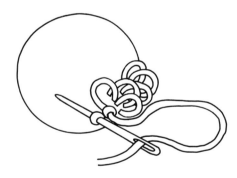

Fig 1   Looped stitch beard

RACING DRIVER HEAD WITH HELMET

Using 3¼mm needles and black yarn for helmet, cast on 5sts. First row, inc 1 st at each end of row. Work 1 row st st. Next row, k1 st black, then join in pink yarn for face for next 5 sts, ending with final stitch in black. Repeat for next row. Next row, knit 2 black, 3 pink, 2 black. Next row, knit

all black. Next row, dec 1 st at each end of row. Repeat for next row. Cut off yarn, leaving 20cm (8in) for sewing in and thread through remaining 3 stitches to fasten off.

This head can also be used on a finger puppet (see below).

MAKING UP

Commence at the top of the head and sew the hair part only firmly in place on garment using same coloured yarn. Should bunches or plaits be required, they should be added at this point. To do this, simply cut 8 or 10 lengths of yarn approximately 6cm (2¼in) long in a matching colour and lay across and under head – ie, between head and garment – prior to stuffing (Fig 2). For stuffing, use a suitable washable material – pieces of old tights or wadding are good – and push firmly into the head, making a good raised and firm shape. Then stitch the remainder of the head into place, remembering to change colour of yarn where necessary.

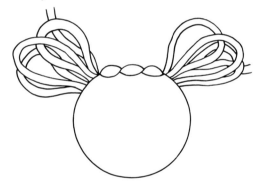

Fig 2   Attaching pigtails

FINGER PUPPETS

When making finger puppets, only one size is required. The instructions that follow are for the making of a basic person, and a simple duck and crocodile in st st using 3¼mm needles and either cotton or wool as preferred.

PERSON

Cast on 9 sts using any colour yarn. Work 6 rows st st. Next row, dec 1 st at each end of row. Repeat for next row, leaving 5 sts. Next row, change to skin-coloured yarn. Next row, inc 1 st at each end of row. Work 2 more rows in st st. Next row, join

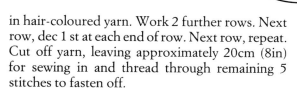

in hair-coloured yarn. Work 2 further rows. Next row, dec 1 st at each end of row. Next row, repeat. Cut off yarn, leaving approximately 20cm (8in) for sewing in and thread through remaining 5 stitches to fasten off.

Repeat the process, finishing with two matching sides.

MAKING UP

Sew in all loose ends. With matching yarn sew together both pieces commencing at the bottom, but leave bottom open. Sew only as far as the hairline on both sides, then if bunches or plaits are required, insert these at this time before completing sewing up. Stuff the head using a suitable washable fabric and tie tightly at neck with matching yarn. With darning needle, sew in eyes and curly hair if required.

DUCK

Follow the instructions for making the 'Person' above, this time using yellow yarn. For the beak, cast on 1 st. First row, knit into front and back of stitch. Next row, repeat (4 sts). Work 2 rows st st. Next row, k2 tog twice. Next row, k2 tog. Cut off yarn, thread through remaining stitch to fasten off.

MAKING UP

Make up following the instructions for the 'Person' above. For beak, fold knitted piece in half, stitch along fold and attach this edge to duck (Fig 3).

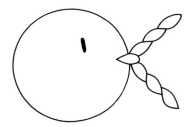

Fig 3   Duck finger puppet

CROCODILE

LOWER JAW

Using green yarn, either cotton or wool, cast on 9 sts and work 8 rows st st. Dec 1 st at each end of

next row and following alternate row. Work 2 rows st st. Next row, dec 1 st at each end. Work 4 rows st st on remaining 3 sts. Cast off.

UPPER JAW

Knit as for lower jaw but work 12 rows before decreasing.

MOUTH

Using red yarn, cast on 3 sts and work 4 rows st st. Inc 1 st at each end of next row and following 4th row. Work 6 rows st st. Dec 1 st at each end of next row. Work 3 rows st st. Dec 1 st at each end of next row. Work 3 rows st st on remaining 3 sts. Cast off.

MAKING UP

Sew together straight sides at neck edge of upper and lower jaw, commencing at cast-on edge and make tuck for the 4 extra rows on upper jaw. Hold tuck in place by stitching right across. Make 2 eyes at bottom of tuck. Place mouth inside jaws, wrong sides together and stitch together using white thread. Then chain stitch with white yarn all around the inside of mouth, working from green side. The stitching on the red mouth gives a good impression of teeth (Fig 4).

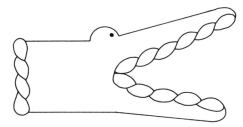

Fig 4   Crocodile

BASIC DOLL

Using skin-coloured double-knitting wool, cast on 9 sts, then work 10 rows st st. Next row, cast on 4 sts and work to end of row. Next row, cast on 4 sts and work to end of row. Next row, cast off 6 sts and work to end of row. Next row, repeat previous row (5 sts remain). Next row, inc 1 st at each end of row. Work 3 rows st st. Change to hair colour, work 2 rows st st. Next row, dec 1 st at each end of row. Next row, repeat previous row.

Cut off yarn, leaving approximately 20cm (8in) for sewing in and thread through remaining stitches and fasten off. Repeat process to make second side.

DOLL VARIATIONS
When making 'Old Man' doll, knit whole doll in skin colour.

MAKING UP
Sew together both sides of doll until hair-line is reached. Insert short lengths of hair-coloured yarn, leaving sufficient at both sides for making bunches or plaits. Then continue to sew together head until complete. Stuff doll's head firmly with washable wadding and tie neck firmly with piece of yarn. Stuff body in similar fashion, not bothering about arms. Sew up bottom of body, stitch in eyes and mouth, fit ribbons to bunches. For 'Old Man' doll, make loop stitches using darning needle and grey yarn around lower part of head for hair and around chin for beard.

JUMPER

Cast on 10 sts in required colour yarn and work 11 rows st st. Cast off. Repeat process to make second side. These jumpers may be made either plain, fancy or striped or in garter stitch (every row knit) if preferred.

MAKING UP
Stitch sides together, leaving open slots for arms and neck.

ANIMALS IN FABRICS

Using either of the animals shown or those of your own choice, make a template from tracing paper and pin on to the materials to be used (Fig 5). If the animals will need to be washed, then use a washable cotton fabric. However, if this is not the case, then I find coloured felt makes an ideal alternative. Cut two squares of either material, slightly larger than the template, plus a square of washable padding of equal size. Sandwich the padding between the materials, pin on the template and stitch all round, using the zigzag attachment on the sewing-machine. Tear off the template and trim with sharp scissors. Using coloured cottons, stitch in details such as eyes or stripes.

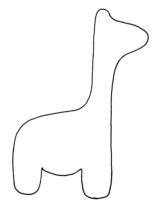

Fig 5   Template for animals

7
THEMES

The idea of producing a series of themes is to demonstrate the ease with which any idea – and I do mean *any* idea – can be used to make a garment of individuality. To prove this point, six completely different subjects have been selected. Each subject has been drawn out in graph form, and, using a basic pattern from Chapter 3, has been turned into a most decorative and appealing garment that reflects the atmosphere and mood of each theme with the help of the theme glossaries and the Picture Library the sky is the limit as far as designs go! Each theme can translate into dozens of different designs that are suitable for adults and children. A single item from the design can be used in making matching socks, mittens or a hat to complete your outfit.

Excluding 'Christmas', the only connection the other subjects have in common is that they feature colourful and bold outdoor places or events. They are 'Seascape', 'City Skylines', 'Carnival', 'Countryside' and 'Jungle' and were selected as themes as I considered that they represented as sufficiently a strong challenge as one is likely to meet, without becoming a designer's nightmare.

Out of my mind's-eye view of New York came 'City Skylines'. Here, displayed on a garment pattern and in the City Skyline glossary, are such features as skyscrapers, yellow taxis, the Statue of Liberty and other landmarks that are associated with that mind's-eye view. Although New York happens to be the featured city, this is purely a personal choice. If Paris, Sydney or London is your choice, then a start may be made using the representative landmarks shown in the City Skyline glossary. Do not be put off by a difficult pattern – for example, St Peter's basilica – as it is easier than it looks.

'Seascape', 'Carnival' and 'Jungle' gave so much pleasure in their creation, not only to me

but also to my outworkers who knitted my designs, choosing their own colours. Generally they felt disappointed when they came to the end of a garment as they had experienced so much fun and enjoyment in watching the story of each pattern unfold. This indicated to me that the correct choice of subject had been made.

When I started drawing up ideas for 'Seascape', I would have loved to have had more space than is available to show all the possibilities of this subject. Just looking at those deep-sea monsters, tropical fish and lumps of coral makes my fingers itch for graph paper and pencil!

Both 'Carnival' and 'Jungle' were great fun to do, although they were somewhat more of a challenge. Attempts to make a monkey resemble a monkey or a dragon a dragon can sometimes end up far from the mark, but in this instance both monkey and dragon look the part and thankfully they ended up in their correct themes. To give these two themes a completely different look, try 'Carnival' on a lighter background to make it a daytime event and 'Jungle' on a darker background for a really dense jungle feeling.

By contrast to these colourful and busy themes, 'Christmas' and 'Countryside' take on a slightly more quiet and sober appearance as befits these subjects. 'Countryside', although retaining its jolly aspect, has a more tranquil look that can only be described as peaceful, and the choice of colours here reflects that peacefulness. 'Christmas', on the other hand, represents all that time means to me, especially family unity.

No matter which theme is selected it is hoped that, given time, they will all feature as part of your wardrobe and I guarantee immense pleasure in their knitting. If, at the beginning, a featured theme is used, I hope that it will not be long before you will be inspired to create garments of your own with very different designs.

CITY SKYLINES

Having had a fascination for buildings, monuments, bridges and so on, since my childhood, I suppose it was only a matter of time before replicas of these began to feature among my designs.

Finding a starting point can often present a problem. You can begin by looking at buildings, monuments and bridges of distinction, or recalling places and buildings from the past that you remember with affection. If you ask anyone to conjure up a vision of Paris, London or Moscow they can always do so as each city has its own definitive style, ambiance and skyline and it is these skylines that make colourful and fascinating jumpers, especially when they are used as an all-round pattern. Our design, with its helicopter, yellow taxi, skyscrapers and Statue of Liberty couldn't be anywhere except New York. You can feel the excitement of the city as you put the cardigan on! See the photo on page 74 for the finished design.

INSTRUCTIONS

The graphs depicting the New York city skyline are shown only in the smallest adult size. When knitting either the medium or large size, refer to the basic pattern shown in Chapter 3, remembering to add extra stitches equally to both sides of the graphs where necessary.

The subject fits easily on to all of the children's jumpers simply by making a slight reduction in the size of the skyscrapers and using the smaller version of the Statue of Liberty shown in the City Skyline glossary. A selection of smaller figures, including the helicopter, can be found in the Picture Library.

Far right Lorenzo and Hannah are both wearing the 'City Skyline' cardigan. *Right* The back in a different colourway. The graph for Lorenzo's cardigan is featured on the following pages and uses the basic cardigan pattern.

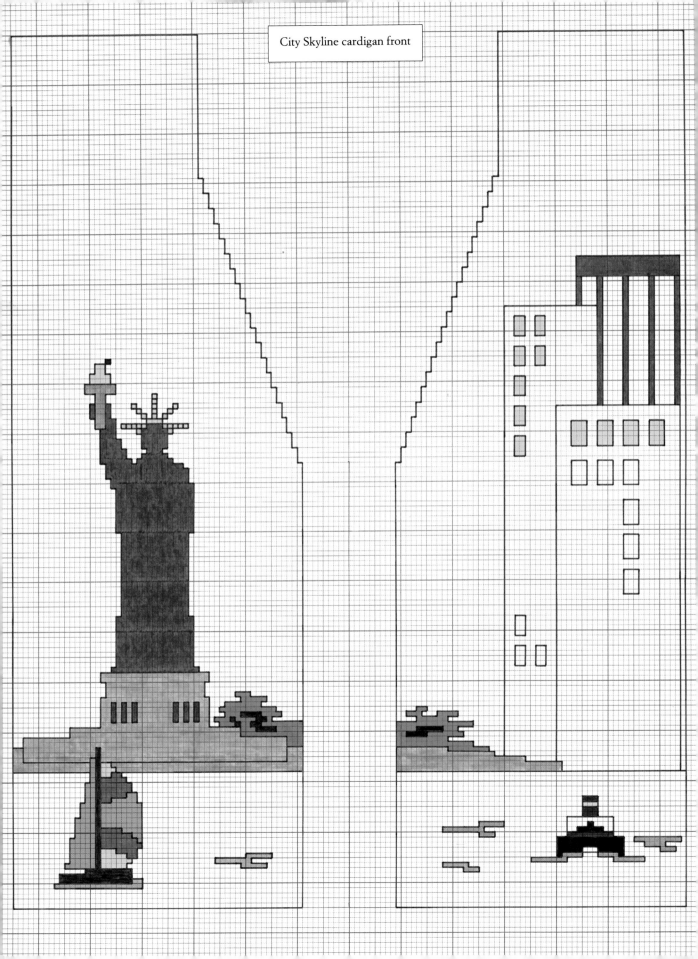

City Skyline cardigan front

City Skyline cardigan back

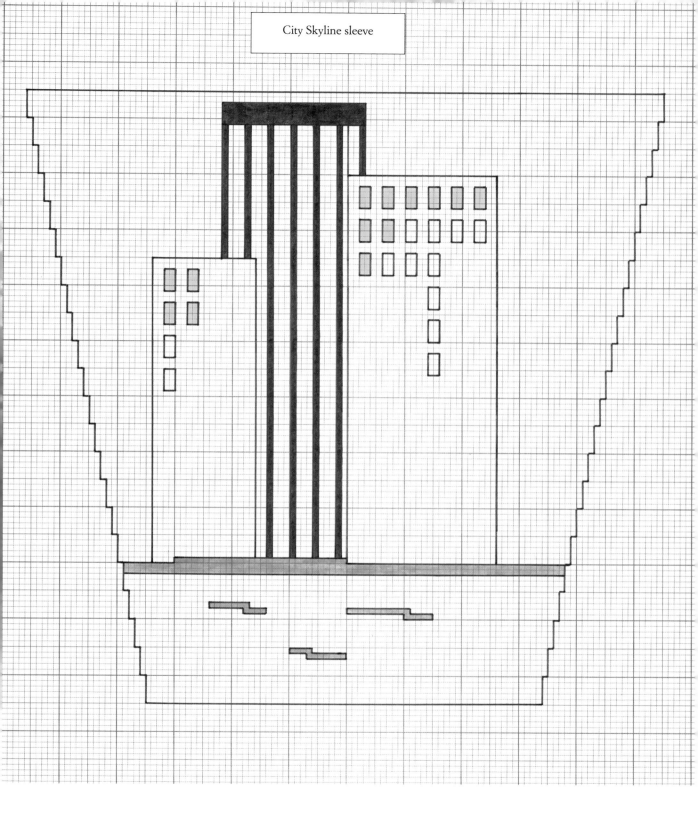

Left I have used the City Skyline cardigan graph but
made it into a crew neck rib bottom jumper.

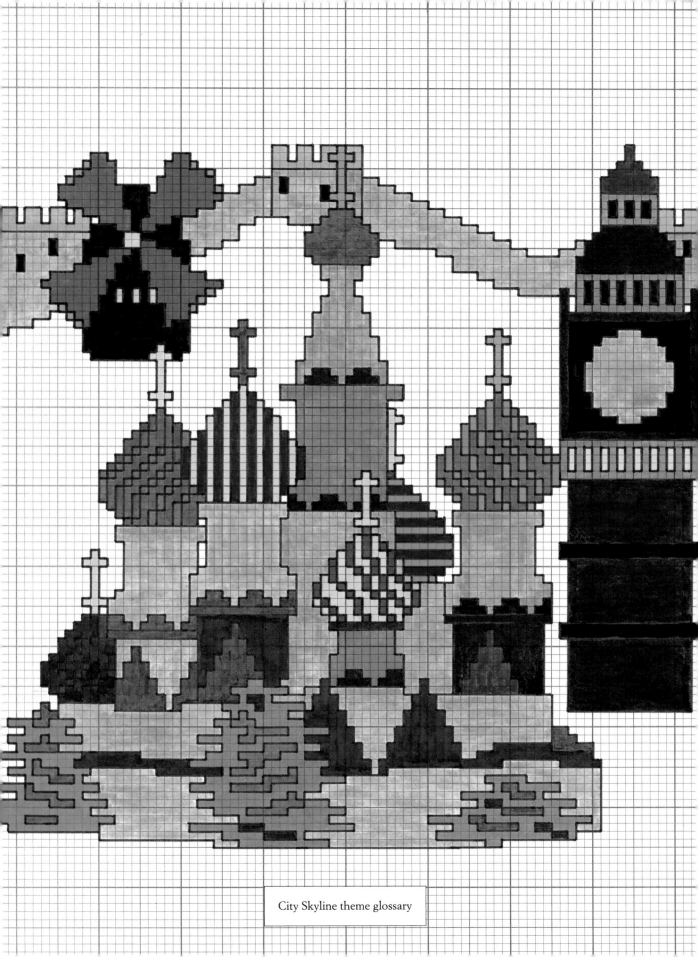

City Skyline theme glossary

SEASCAPE

When I designed this garment, not only did it give me much pleasure and fun, but also greater freedom than normal. For instance, the use of cotton yarns with their very varied and vibrant colours helps to give a real feel of the sea. They certainly give an air of clarity that is in keeping with sailing the estuaries on a fine day and at the same time display the exotic undersea world of a Pacific island.

As the glossary of the sea shows, much enjoyment was also had in creating the undersea monsters. Here my imagination and colour co-ordination ran wild! It is not difficult to imagine the look of a garment that features one of these monsters, especially when enlarged to cover the whole area of both front and back. Using the exotic colours available, it would be a sensation of colour when displayed on a subdued background, and would be a talking point when worn.

On both child and adult garments shown far right, the use of border patterns can be seen to great effect.

INSTRUCTIONS

The design featured here in graph form is that of the smallest child size, using cotton yarn and crew neck with rib bottom pattern. To knit for medium and large child size, simply add the extra stitches necessary equally to both sides of each graph section. Instructions for making the two dolls are to be found on page 66.

When knitting adult versions, use designs from the seascape glossary and Picture Library.

Far right Ben, Hannah and Sian's 'Seascape' jumpers used the crew neck and rib bottom pattern. Hannah's design is shown in graph form on the following pages. Ben's jumper has fishes from the seascape glossary.
Right This picture shows the effective continuation of the design on the sleeves.

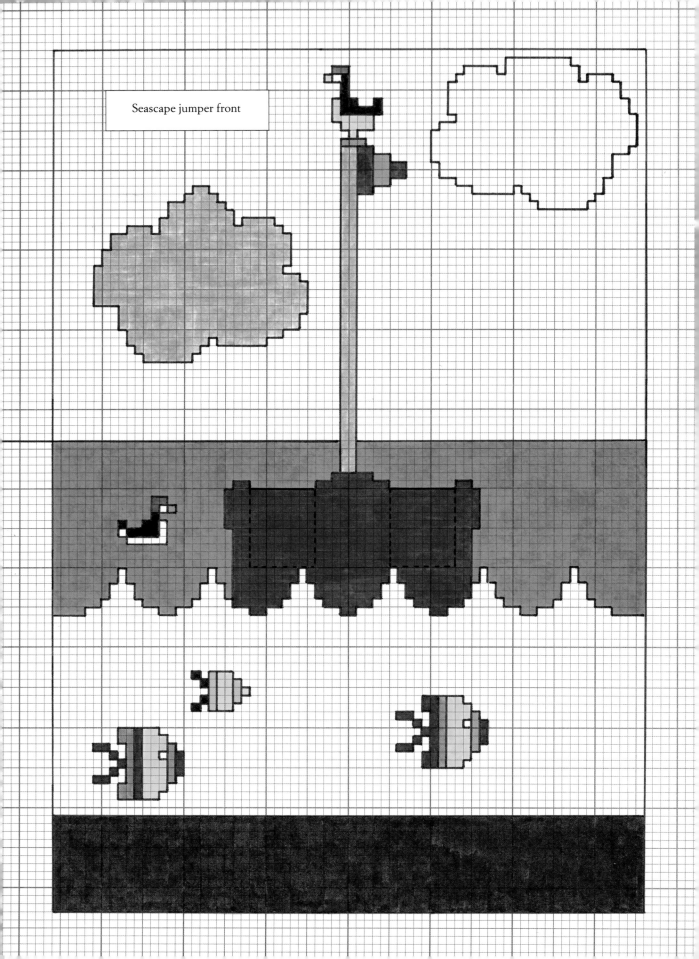

Seascape jumper front

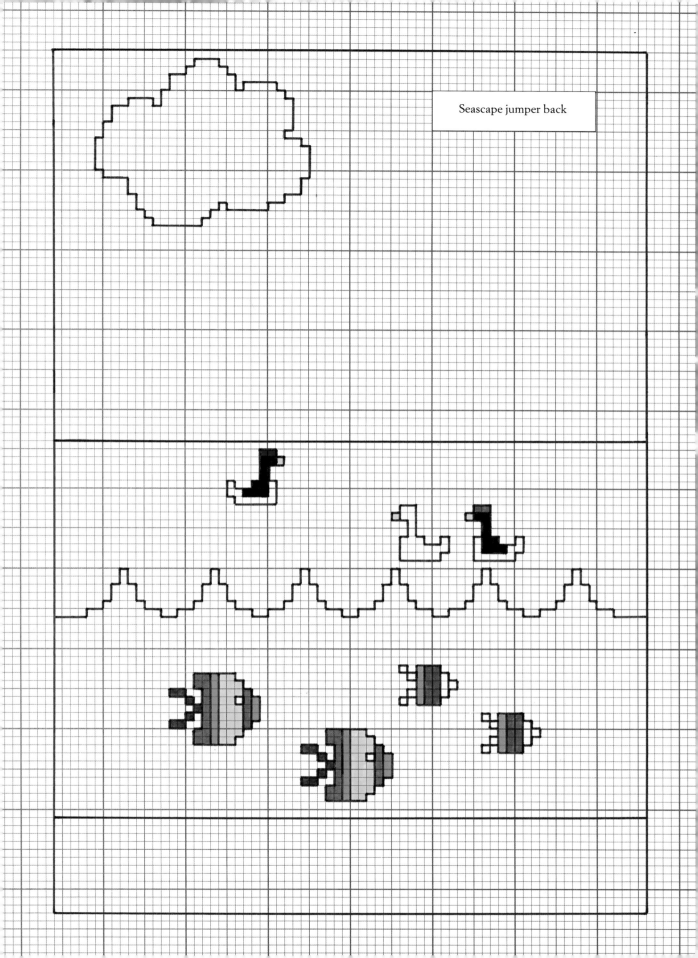

Seascape jumper back

Seascape jumper sleeves
(both the same)
Opposite Seascape theme
glossary

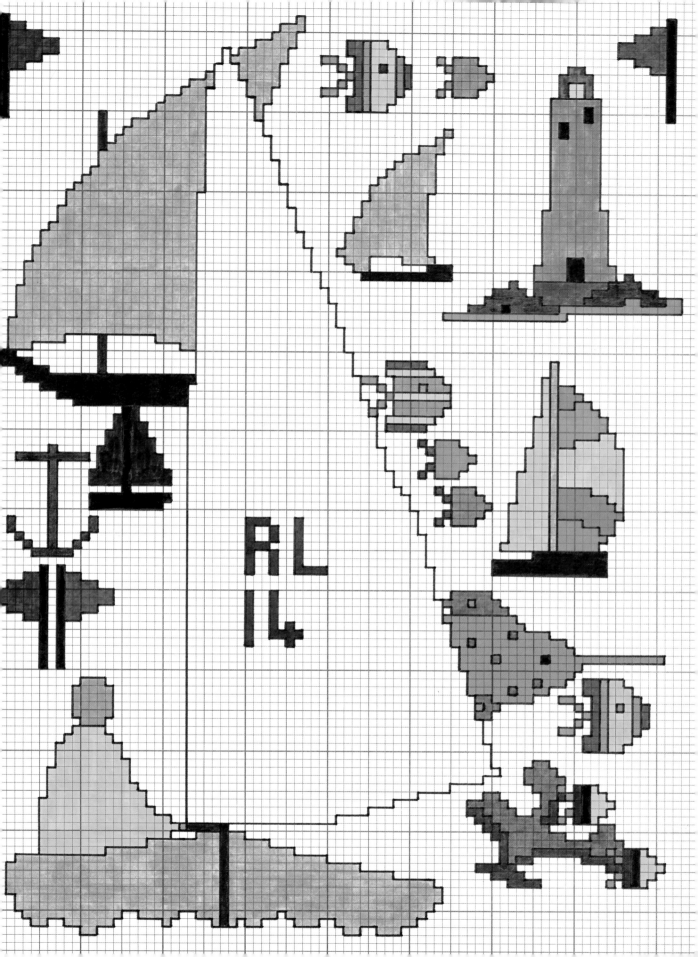

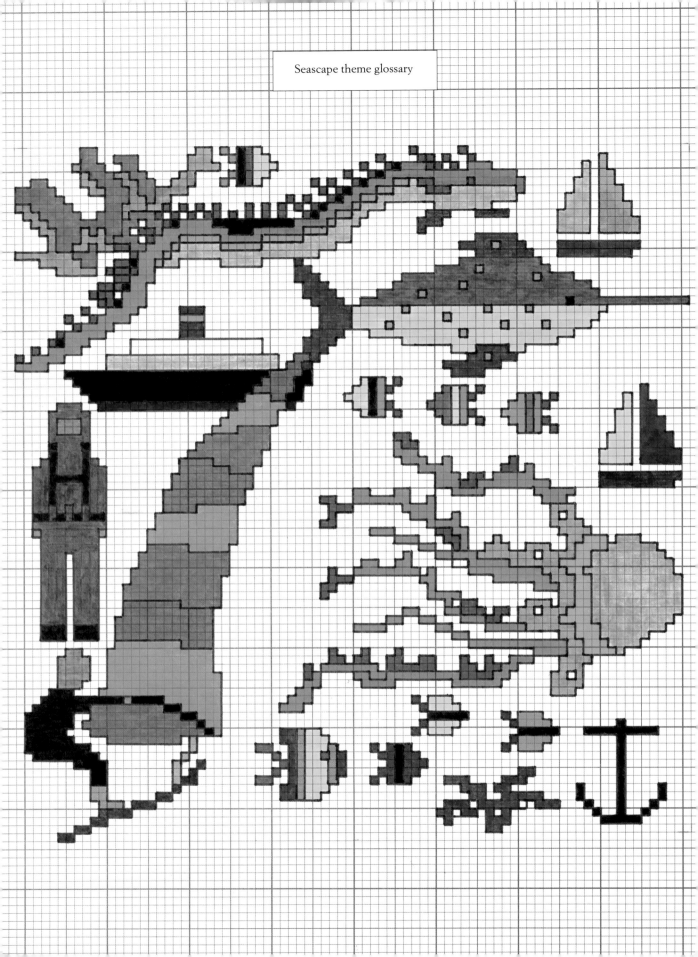

Seascape theme glossary

CHRISTMAS

For most people, Christmas is their favourite calendar event of the year. In my family Christmas holds a special place and even though the children have left home, stockings are still put out on Christmas Eve and the full tradition of Christmas is kept, and I know that this is so in the homes of my children and their families. So what better way to portray Christmas than to have a large family gathered around the tree on Christmas morning as shown on the adult version or two small children peeping around the door to see what Father Christmas has brought them on the child's version? All the subjects that make up this design are shown in the Christmas glossary, with further material available from the Picture Library. I feel, however, that the family will take on a strong resemblance to your own.

INSTRUCTIONS

The graphs shown are for the smallest child size and are featured in two colourways for hand-knitting: royal/black, and an identical version in cream/bottle for machine knitting. When making a garment for medium and large child sizes, add the extra stitches required equally to both sides of the graph.

When making stuffed heads for people in doorway, see page 66.

To make parcels for the tree, cast on 5 stitches with 3¼mm needles, work 6 rows in st st, cast off and attach to the tree with brightly coloured ribbons.

Ben is wearing a machine-knitted version of the Christmas jumper shown on page 86 and the hat from page 52.

Here are two ideas for a Christmas design. The pattern
used is crew neck with rib bottom and graphs for
Hannah's version are on the following pages. A machine
knitted version is shown on page 85.

Christmas jumper front

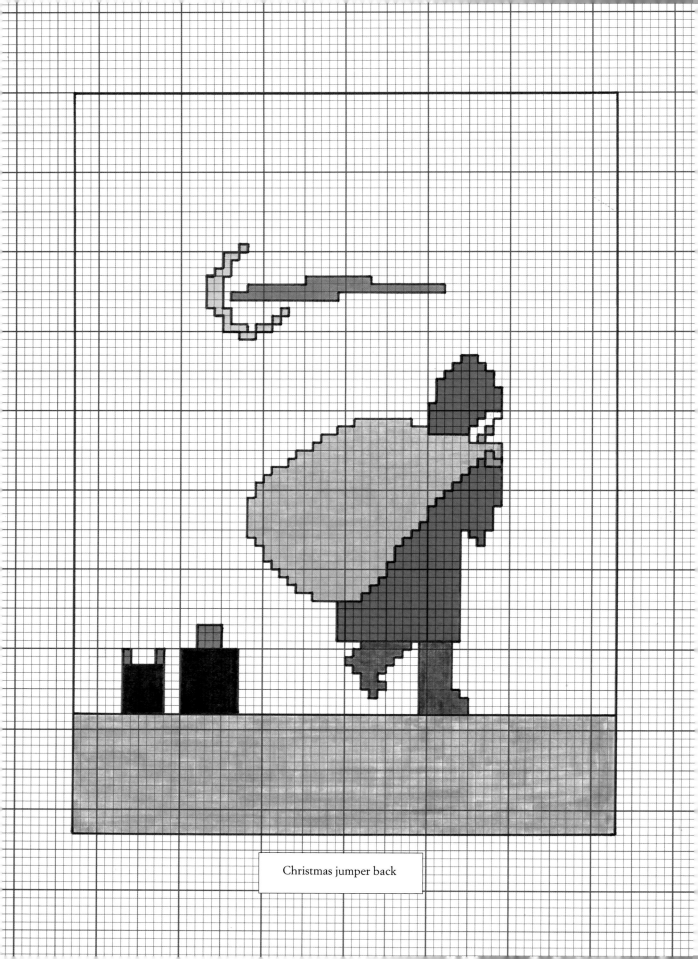

Christmas jumper back

Christmas jumper sleeves
(both the same)

COUNTRYSIDE

As I live and work in an olde worlde cottage, deep among the sounds, sights and smells of the countryside, a garment that displays this way of life was inevitable. To be surrounded by a rural environment does increase your awareness of the seasons' changes, and I have endeavoured to convey an idea of this by designing a garment that has, on one side, a look of springtime, and on the other, the feel of autumn. Both scenes are equally at home sitting side by side on the same garment and are very much in keeping for the time of year when a warm jumper is likely to be needed.

A child's version is easily designed, using items from the glossary. A tractor ploughing or a field of corn with our scarecrow in residence are ideal. I particularly like the idea of the colours in this theme reflecting the muted shades of the countryside. However, a few bright contrasts, carefully used, add exciting impact.

Handy hint Single swiss-darned stitches in white make realistic birds.

INSTRUCTIONS

The graph shows the jumper in the smallest adult size using the roll-neck, tunic bottom pattern and to this I have added a simple pattern of diamonds, knitted in reverse st st to hem and sleeves.

When knitting the medium and large size garments, be sure to carry the tree design to the extreme edges of seams.

Far right 'Countryside' worn by Sian uses the roll neck with tunic bottom pattern. *Right* The back emphasises its spring and autumn features. The graphs for this theme are shown on the following pages.

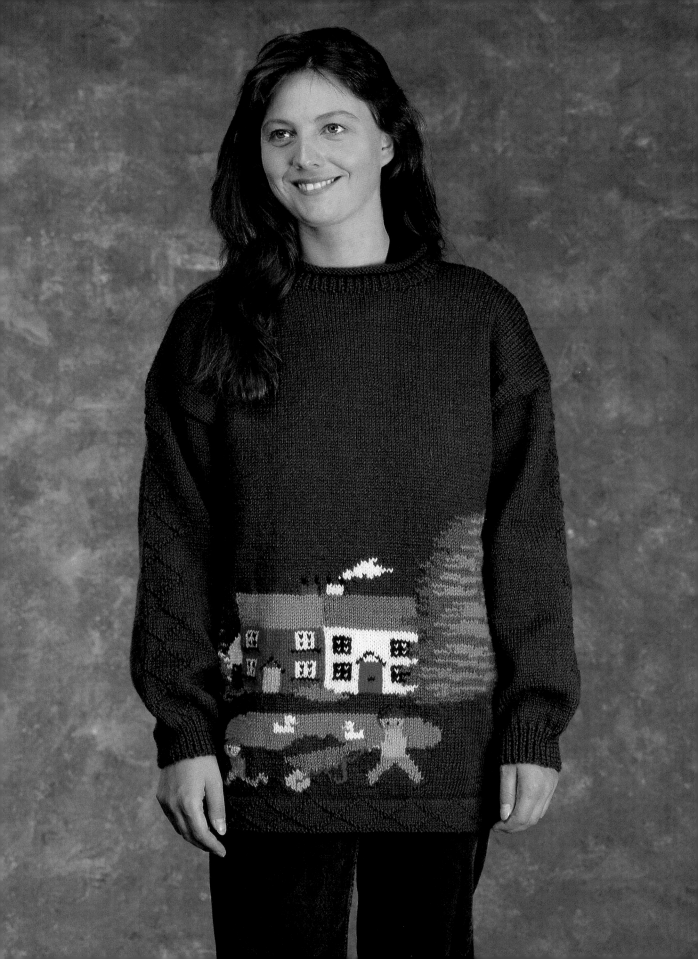

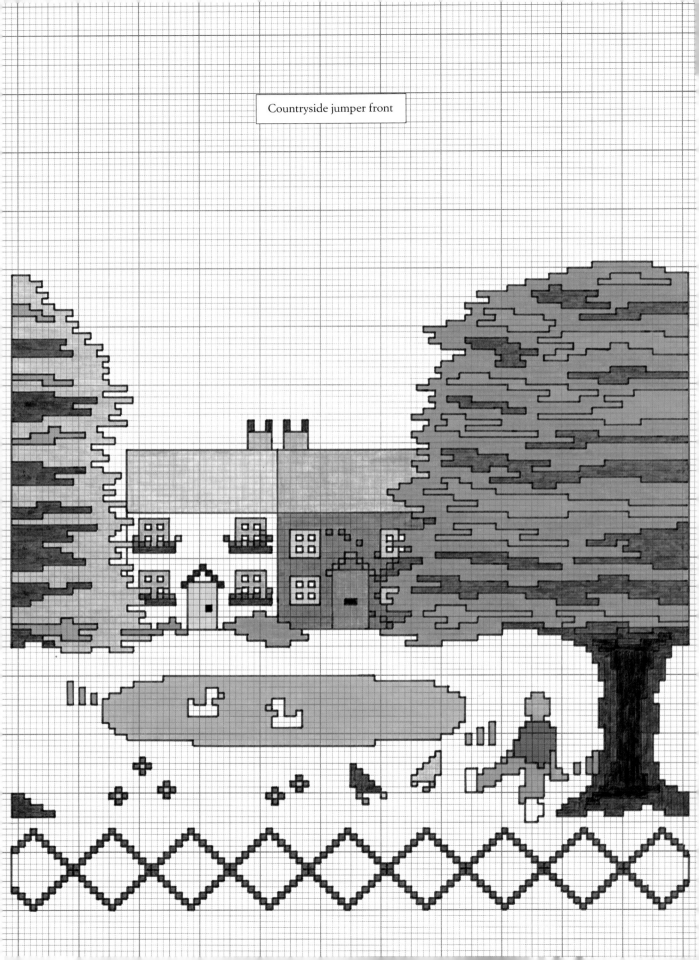

Countryside jumper front

Countryside jumper back

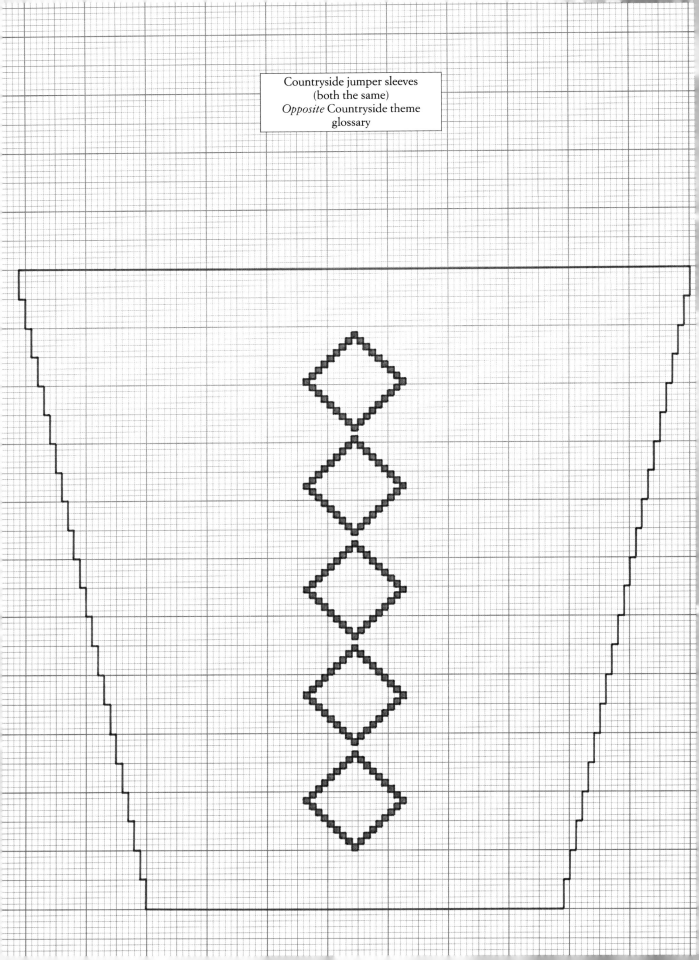

Countryside jumper sleeves
(both the same)
Opposite Countryside theme
glossary

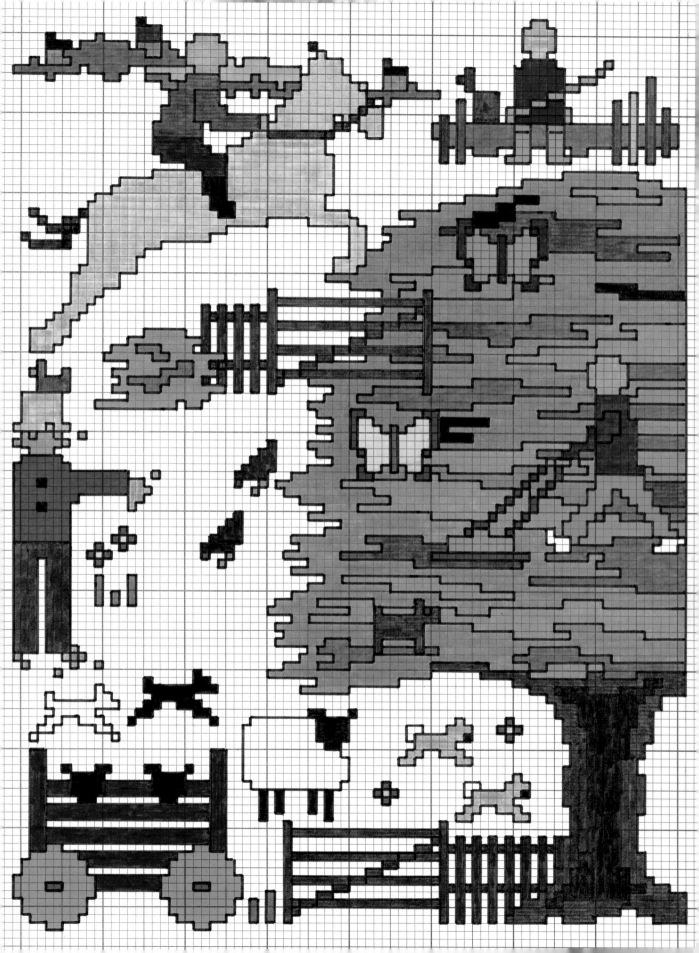

Countryside theme glossary

CARNIVAL

Soon after deciding that a carnival was to feature as one of my themes, I realised that I had presented myself with a serious problem. Not wishing to change my decision cost me a small mountain of graph paper and not a small amount of time!

Carnivals are big, brassy, noisy and colourful, in equal amounts and always much larger than life. To turn all this into a design frustrated me for a while. Picturing floats adorned by pretty ladies in fantastic plumes did not really appeal, especially if detail was to be sacrificed to a welter of colour. This was not what I wished to portray. So my design became a dragon, which wound itself around the garment in a circular splash of colour, leaving the head to display detail. Having mentioned border patterns earlier, this I felt was the ideal place for its use. So a Chinese dragon, adorned with lanterns and Chinese fireworks, became a China Town carnival for the Chinese New Year.

INSTRUCTIONS

The graphs shown are for the smallest size and use the roll neck tunic bottom pattern. The border pattern of Chinese lanterns is incorporated into the hem. When knitting medium and large size patterns, simply extend dragon and lanterns to edges as required.

Right The back view of the dragon. Graphs for this theme are shown on the following pages. *Overleaf* 'Carnival' shows off to perfection the use of vibrant colours and is knitted in the roll neck tunic bottom pattern.

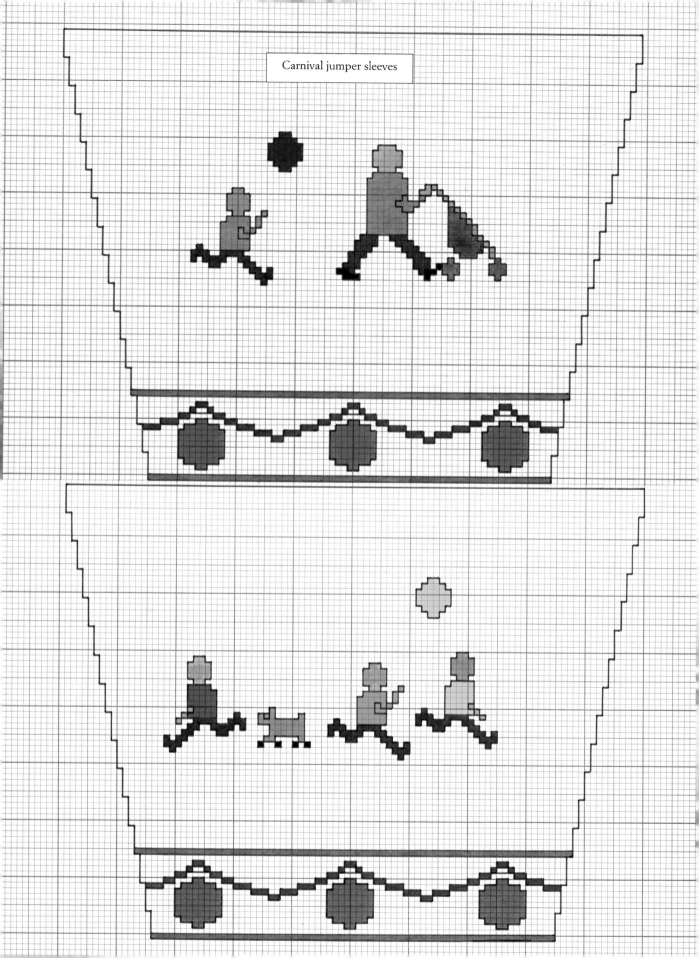

Carnival jumper sleeves

Carnival jumper back

Carnival jumper front

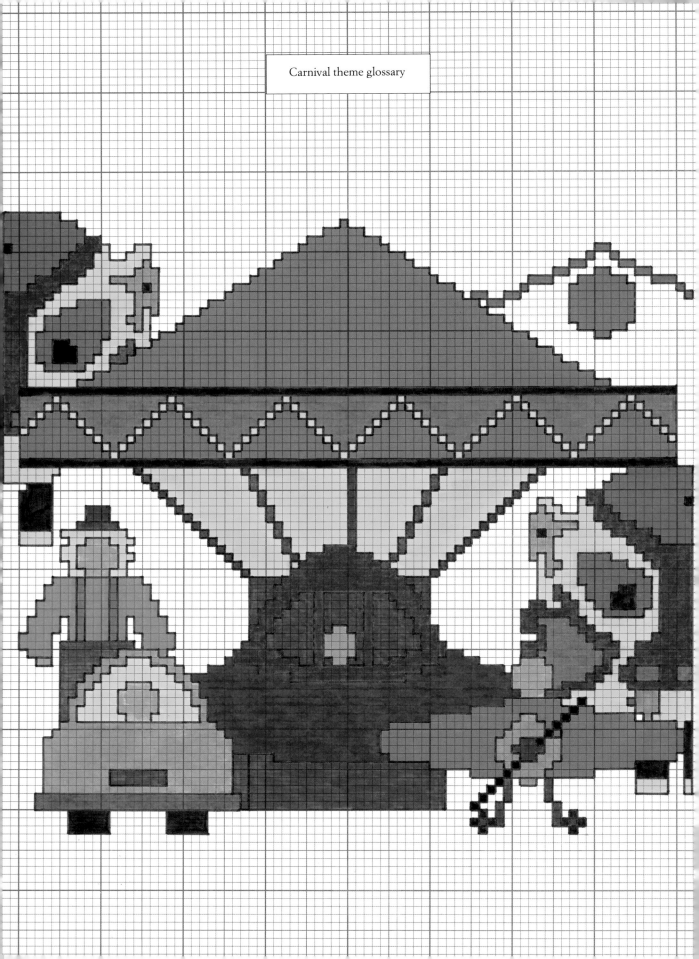

Carnival theme glossary

JUNGLE

The word 'jungle' has many interpretations and is often used to describe such places as a rain forest, a wilderness, a dense thicket and even modern-day business centres, conveyed by the term 'concrete jungle'. I use the word frequently, especially when searching through my workshop for the elusive ball of wool known to be lurking somewhere among its dark and dingy recesses. All these interpretations, with the exception of the workshop, would make fine picture jumpers and, given time, may one day form part of a collection.

This jungle scene garment for adults leans towards the rain forest idea with its luxurious growth of green vegetation and exotic flowers. So it is possible that one idea has been used up, although there are plenty more to choose from.

As in the real rain forest, monkeys abound and although I'm not too sure where tigers come from, they look quite at home here. With their distinctive stripes and cuddly appearance, they look very friendly.

INSTRUCTIONS

The graphs show the garment in the smallest adult size, using the crew neck with rib bottom basic pattern. When knitting for medium and large size garments, be sure to carry branch and leaf design to the extreme edge of seams.

The children's jungle garment incorporates designs taken from the Jungle glossary and Picture Library.

When making stuffed heads for monkeys, knit the smallest head as described on page 66, using suitably matching yarn.

Far right Sian and Hannah are wearing different designs of the 'Jungle' theme. I feel Hannah's is more suitable for a child. Sian's version is displayed in graph form in the following pages. Both jumpers are in the crew neck rib bottom pattern. *Right* Close up of the boat on Hannah's jumper.

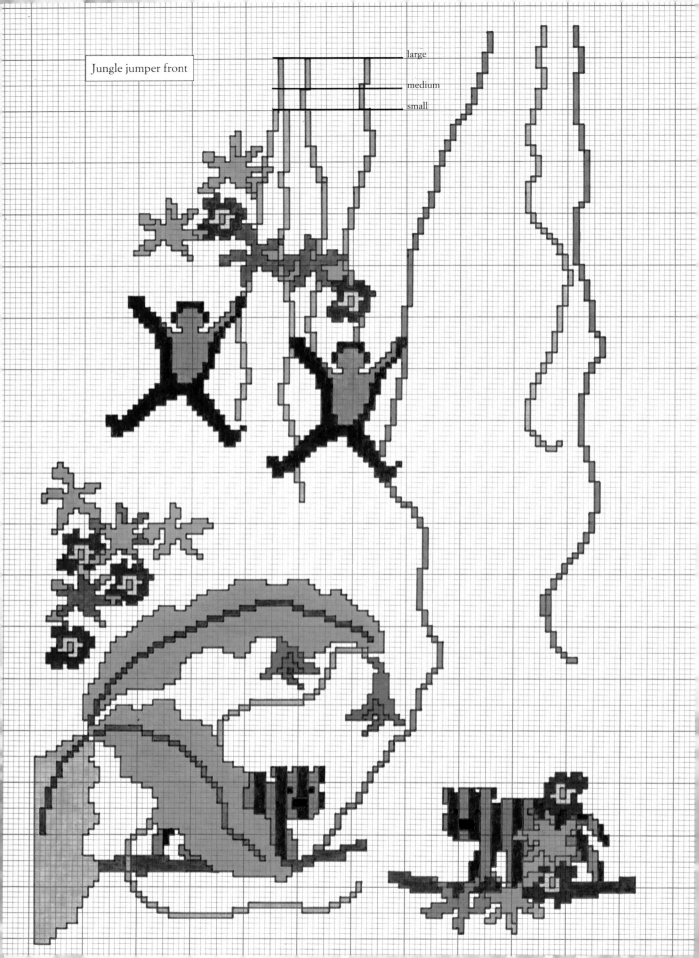

Jungle jumper front

large

medium

small

large

medium

small

Jungle jumper back

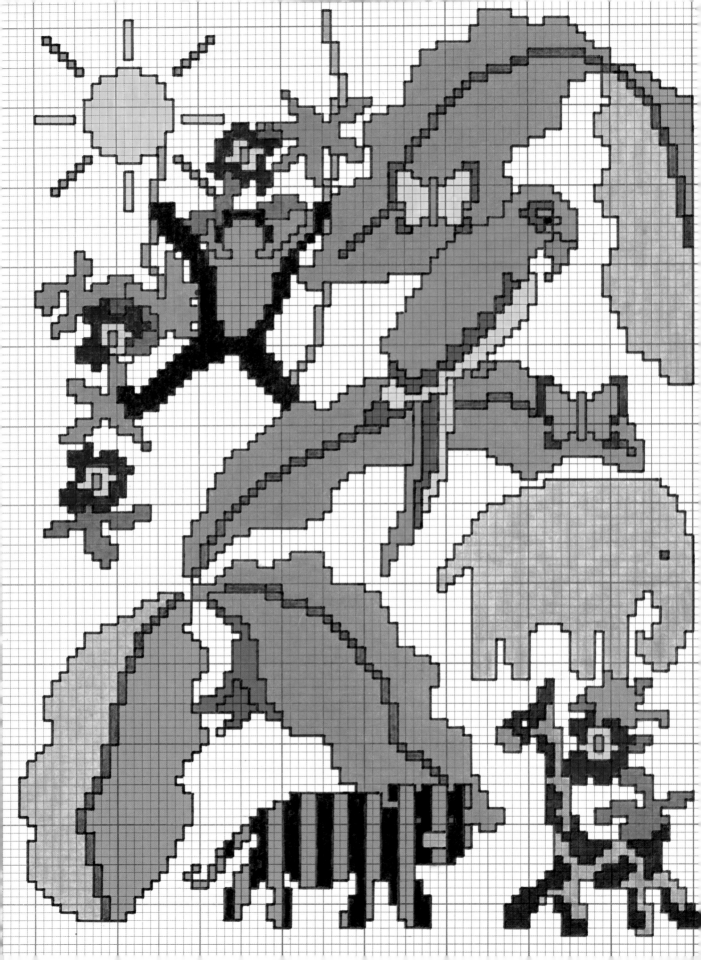

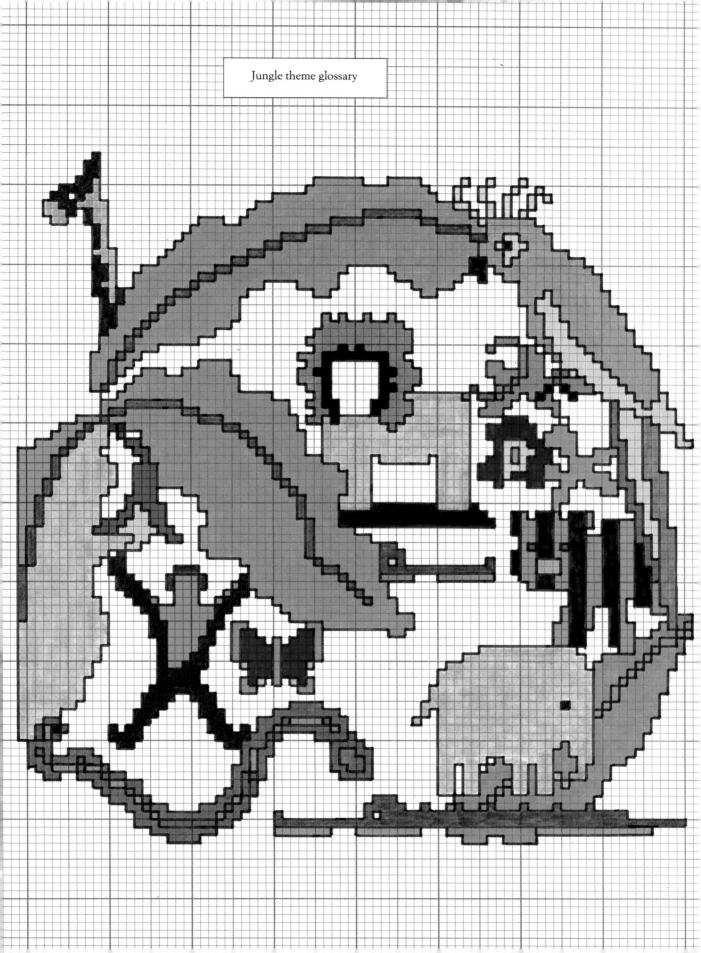

Jungle theme glossary

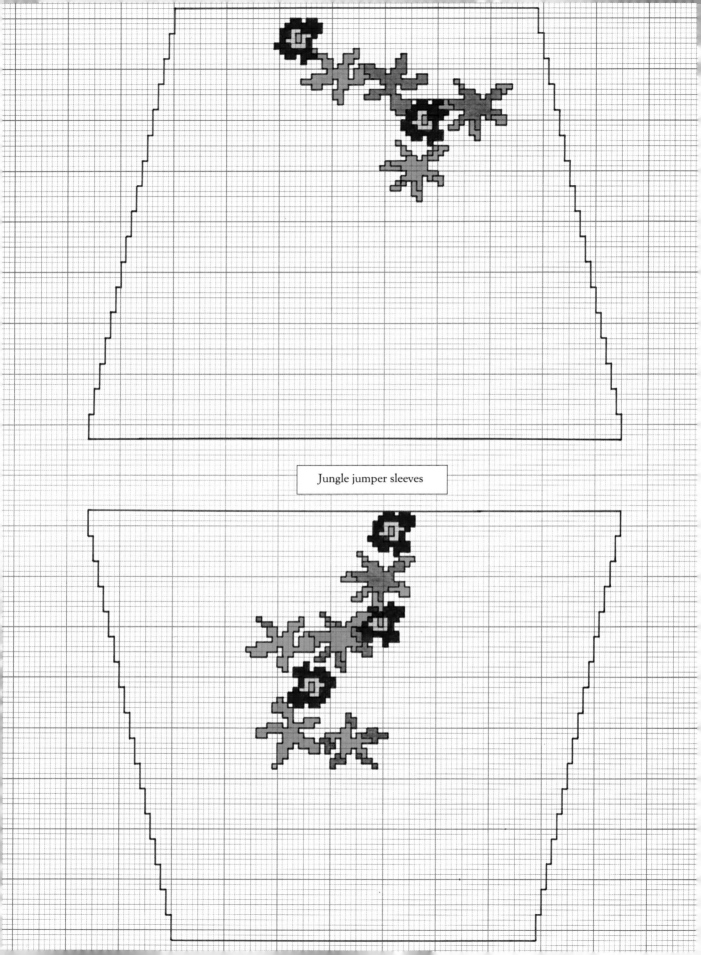

Jungle jumper sleeves

8
PICTURE LIBRARY

To use the library, select any item necessary for your design and, using tracing paper and a soft pencil, transfer the item on to your graph.

When compiling a library, the biggest problem is having to decide what to include and what not to include, and in this respect, compiling the library for this book was no different. However, I do hope a correct balance has been achieved.

The library has been divided into categories for easier use and each category contains a good selection of items that relate to its designated subject heading. Lack of space has restricted the amount that can be shown, but this should not be a disadvantage as by now you should feel confident in making graphs of your own. Remember, though, that if you are in any doubt about its size and proportions you should knit up the item first before committing it finally to your design.

It is possible to use the library on a mix-and-match basis, either by using some items from the library mixed with items of your own, or by designing the garment entirely from items drawn from the various categories. Either way, if you use the library as a reference, it will not be long before those wonderful picture jumpers are being made to suit your personal needs.

Our unique cot cover is made entirely using alphabet letters from the Picture Library. By rearranging the letters into your family name, the cover could be passed on to other members of the family when outgrown and possibly become a treasured heirloom.

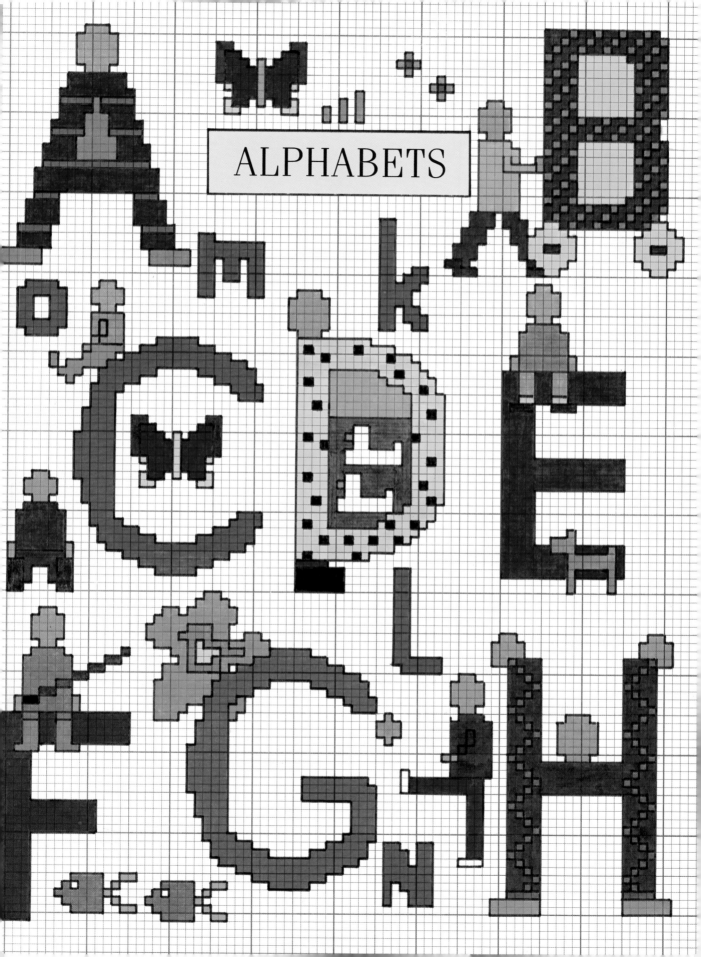

ALPHABETS

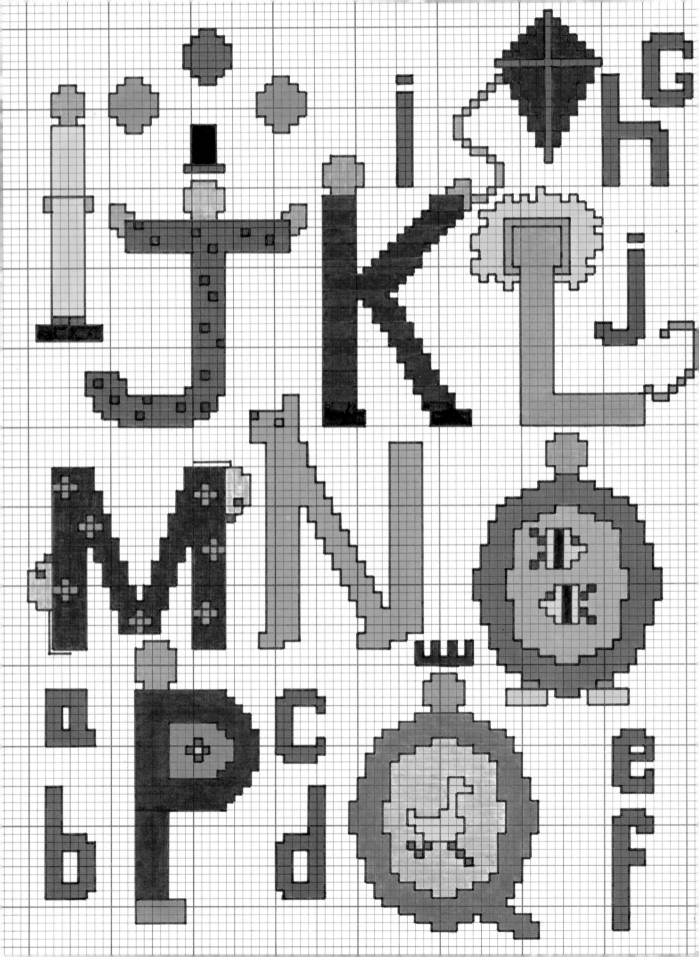

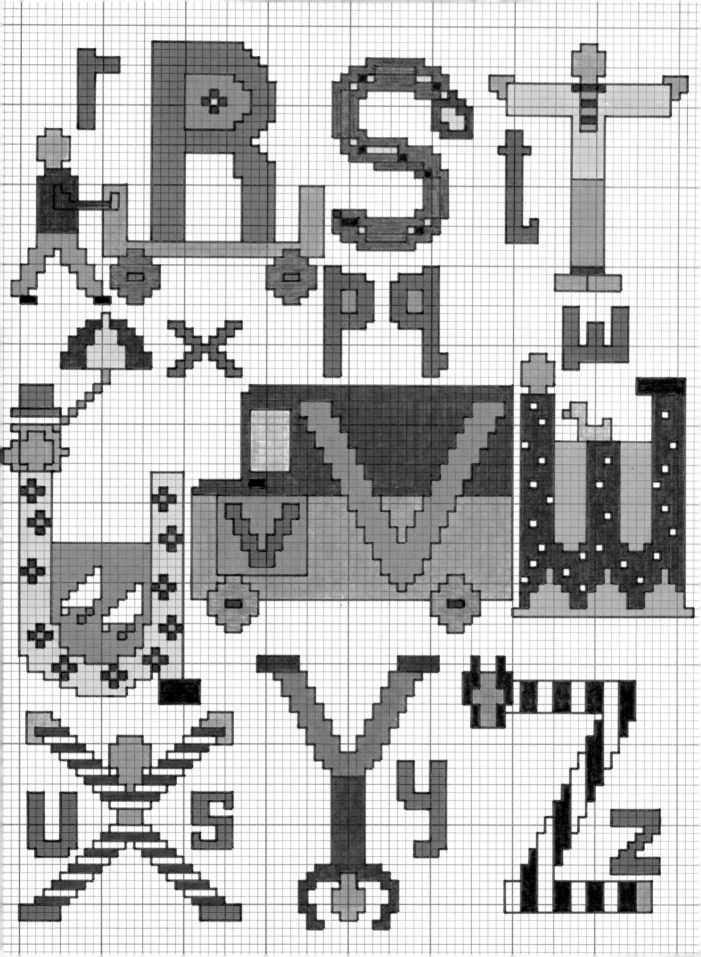

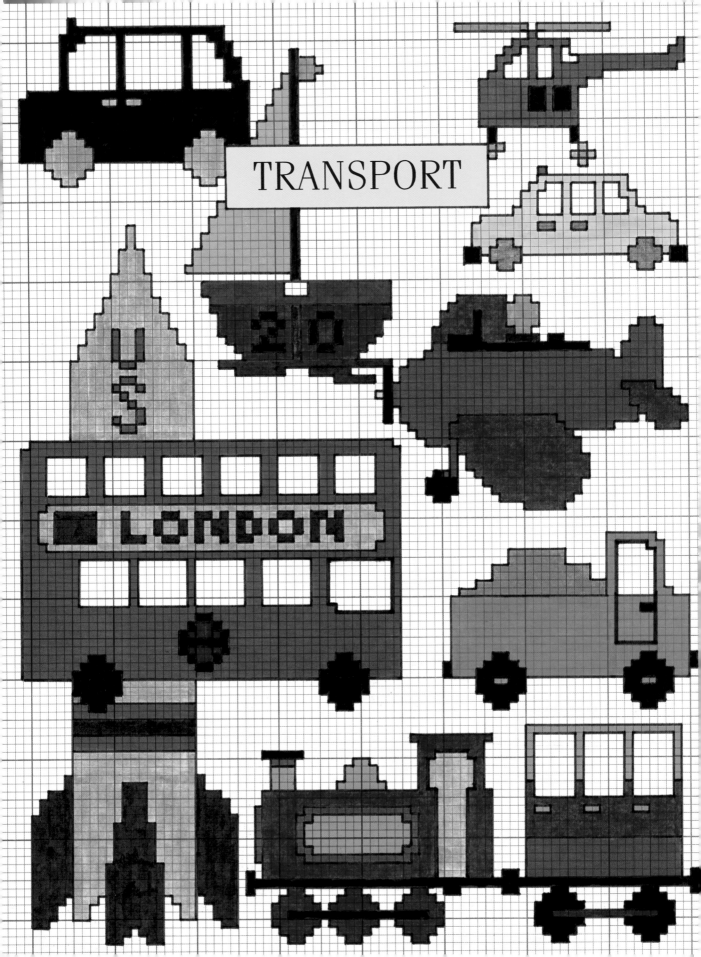

TRANSPORT

LONDON

FLOWERS

PEOPLE

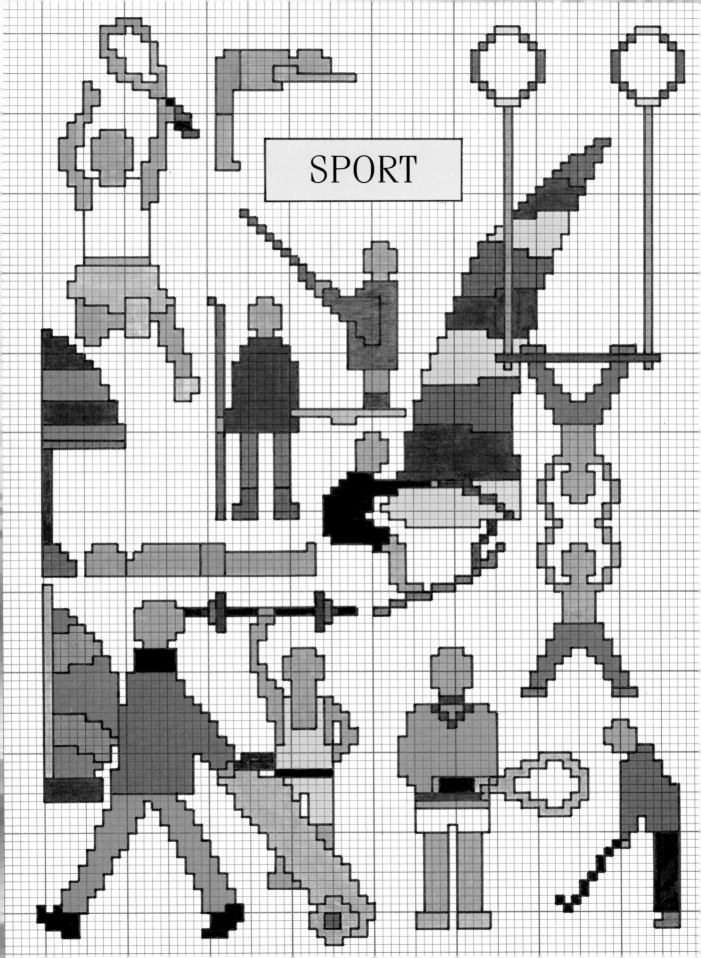

SPORT

TREES

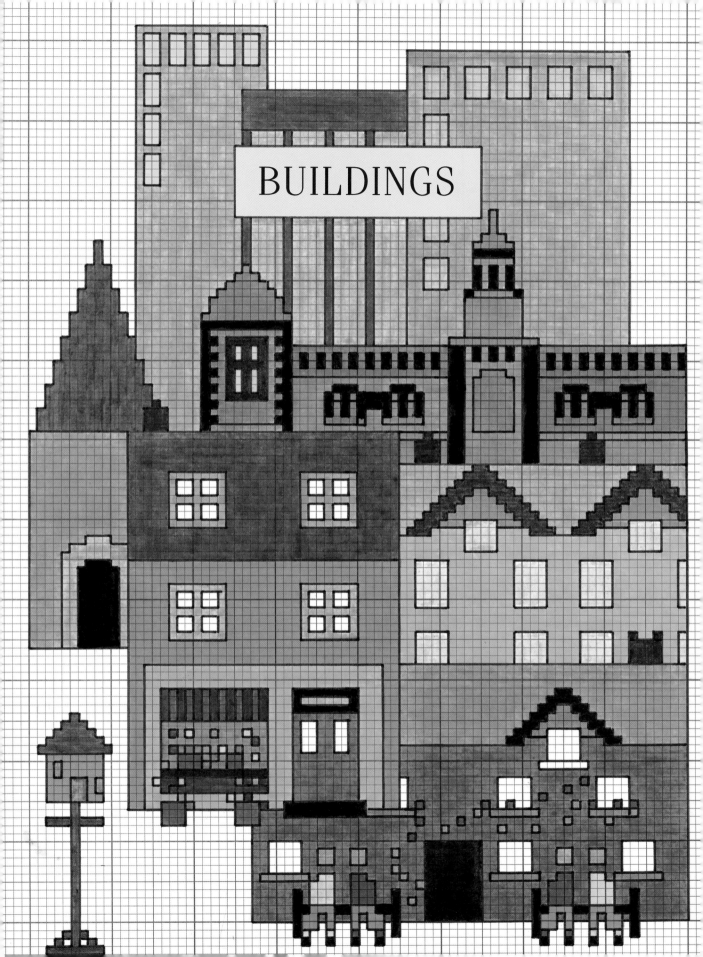

BORDERS

YARN SUPPLIERS

UK Suppliers
Texere Yarns,
College Mill, Barkerend Road, Bradford, West
Yorkshire BD3 9AQ

T. Forsell & Son Ltd,
Blaby Road, South Wigston, Leicester LE8 2SG

Overseas Suppliers
Nomi Lee Yarn,
142 Congressional Lane, Rockville, MD20852,
USA

Westrade Sales Inc,
2711 No 3 Road, Richmond BC, V6X 2B2,
Canada

Pikkusormustin,
Kalliokuja 5, SF-07170, Pornainen, Finland

Projeko,
Raamsingel 30, 2012 DT Haarlem, Netherlands

Jens B. Thomsen,
Strikkeboden, GI Kongevej 161, 1850
Frederiksberg C., Copenhagen, Denmark

K.& F. Sarolla Teo,
Kilmacrenan, Nr Letterkenny, Co Donegal, Eire

Karingal Vic/Tas Pty Ltd
10 Reid Street, Bayswater, Victoria 3153,
Australia

ACKNOWLEDGEMENTS

Frank and I have had enormous fun writing this book and in the process have had tremendous help from a variety of people without whom it would never have seen the light of day. Our special thanks go to:

Alyson Valentine and Maureen Hazelden, not forgetting their long-suffering husbands; Donya Davis, speed knitter extraordinaire; Marjorie Payne; Amanda Lonsdale, for her lovely illustrations; Christopher Lane, computer wizard; Maureen Carr; Carol Woodhams, our knitted-head lady; Betty Rolfes; Christopher, Ben and Hannah Thorpe for their patience at being photographed for hours on end; Texere Yarns in the guise of Robin Smith; Dyed in the Wool; T. Forsell & Son Ltd; Roddy Payne for the photography.

INDEX

Illustrations are shown in **bold** type
Charts are shown in *italics*